THE LAST OF STEAM

THE LAST OF STEAM

A billowing pictorial pageant
of the waning years of steam
railroading in the United States

BY JOE G. COLLIAS

HOWELL-NORTH   San Diego   California

1980 PRINTING

Printed and bound in the United States of America.

Library of Congress Catalogue Card No. 60-14067

Published by Howell-North Books
11175 Flintkote Avenue   San Diego, CA 92121

Table of Contents

Foreword 7

Steam in Transition 9

Great Northern 57

Ore For the Mills of Bethlehem 63

Frisco Spit and Polish 67

Redhots 71

Illinois Central Steam 87

The Mighty Niagara 93

Too Broke to Buy 97

Mike 'n Ike 113

The Displaced EM-1's 117

Burlington, a Granger Road in Steam 125

The Die-Hards 131

Union Pacific — Main Line West 159

Big Boy, Symbol of Survival 177

Espee Steam, Last in the Far West 189

    The Keeler Branch 196

At the Rock of the Cajon 198

Mountains on the Flatlands 201

Smoke in the Red River Valley 209

Along the Atchison, Topeka & Ohio 217

Branch Line to the Coal Fields 223

The Bashful Berkshires 227

She Fell Down on the Hill 231

A Portfolio of Steam 234

Foreword

In his continual search for something better man has devised and created goods and machines that have left more than a passing impression on his generations. It is a credit to our way of life that though these creations are taken for granted by most people, there are always those who possess an undying interest in a creation with which they may never have direct contact. Thus it is that while some gaze rapturously at an aged Mississippi stern wheeler and collect souvenirs of its kind, others spend their lives searching for and collecting postage stamps, coins, and the like from the distant corners of the globe. Antique automobiles, modern airplanes and rockets all come in for their share of attention; in fact, very little that man has created does not gather a following, sometimes momentarily interested spectators or again avid followers whose quest for information and experiences knows no bounds.

No other devising of man created such an enthusiastic following as that of the most nearly human of his creations, the American steam locomotive. Since its inception it has been an object of attention and fascination on the part of the American public. Though its construction and operation are really quite simple, its outside motion and near human laborings have never ceased to arouse amazement and fascination on the faces of onlookers. No other machine has so universally captured the public's imagination and affection. Literally thousands have succumbed to the love of this smoke belching, fire eating machine whose whistles in the night have given rise to songs, ballads, and publications by the hundreds. In fact, a fair share of the American economy may be attributed to the adoration of this machine, as evidenced by the untold number of model steam locomotives built and sold every year not only to adolescents but to numerous scale builders whose basements and attics reek of soot and smoke, scaled down of course to the appropriate size. A considerable sum is spent on photography and its inherent equipment by those who find great pleasure in recording the steam engine on film for posterity.

This species of human who adores such a machine has bestowed upon himself a title of distinction that sets him apart from the station onlookers and gives him a right to criticize and praise. He is a *railfan,* a lover of steam locomotives, first, last, and always.

This book is a railfan's attempt to capture on film the passage of the steam locomotive across the American continent in its final days before extinction. With the close of the Second World War it became increasingly and painfully apparent that the newly developed diesel-electric locomotive was the railroad motive power of the future and in time would replace every steam locomotive in existence. No words are necessary to prove that this belief has been borne out. For the railfan the end of an era has come.

It is not the author's intention to argue the relative merits of either type of motive power or why one has replaced the other. The replacement of diesel over steam has largely been a matter of economics rather than of power or speed, and in a day and age when competition is razor sharp the railroads must grasp at anything that promises economy.

As of this publication, and it was intended to be so, the steam engine is virtually nonexistent on the American continent. The diesel-electric locomotive, a curiosity only 20 years ago, is now the accepted thing, having invaded every railroad terminal in the land. Steam locomotives built only a decade ago have been retired and even the most modern steam power has felt the scrap yard's cutting torch.

It wasn't until 1950 that this wholesale slaughter of the American steam locomotive fleet began in earnest. A few roads had become wholly dieselized by this date, while many others were partially dieselized. The writing was on the wall and managements were setting dates for completing replacement of steam power with diesel-electric. Some roads stuck to their forecasts while others were forced to return again and again to a steam stockpile for seasonal upturns in traffic. Finally even these seasonal returns of steam were doomed. 1960 loomed as the year for complete extinction of the steam locomotive.

This book portrays the steam locomotive in action, in all its glory in the closing days of steam. This is the steam engine as it rolled up the remaining miles and passed into oblivion. It is the steam engine as I and others would like to remember it. This is primarily a photo album with text at a minimum, for who needs words when a little imagination, memory, and a good photograph will bring back unforgettable moments?

The author regrets, and sincerely so, that not all the power that operated into this ten-year period is pictured herein. The elements of time, weather, and ever increasing dieselization prohibited the photography of much that is missed. Much of the beautiful steam power of New England, the South and Far West is missing due to its passing out of existence before arrangements could be made to photograph it.

This is steam from 1950 on. This is the *last* of steam!

JOE G. COLLIAS

Maplewood, Missouri
1960

Steam in Transition

The future of steam was indeed a closed issue by the spring of 1950 what with several of the country's railroads having already killed the fires in their remaining steam power. What was of more importance, however, was the fact that many lines had already cast their votes for internal-combustion power and if not well on the way to complete dieselization had at least invested heavily enough in the newest of motive power to show they meant business.

Policies for operation of both types of motive power varied during this period of predieselization. Some operating departments preferred to congregate all steam power on one division, thus eliminating duplicate servicing facilities on the rest of the system. Others preferred to mix the power system, letting prevailing traffic conditions rule the need for steam. Thus it behooved any railfan who wanted yet another opportunity at sight and sound of steam on these roads to be constantly on his toes for the day when steam would again be in use, albeit temporarily.

Though dieselization on such roads was a certainty, the daily status of steam versus diesel varied constantly. There occurred during this phase several instances, notably in the case of the Rock Island 5100 class 4-8-4's, where steam was allowed a last word before execution, so to speak, when in order to write the cost of recently purchased steam power off the account books a whole class of steam power would be reactivated and used at every opportunity until the financial department felt the cost of the new machinery was justified.

In every case though, these smaller class I roads, notably in the South, East, and Midwest, finished their dieselization program shortly after the turn of the decade. This was the transitional period for railroad motive power. The diesel was no longer an infant; it had proven itself and was firmly established on many fronts. With the fall of steam on these middle of the roaders only the larger carriers and the die-hard holdouts remained. The passage of the steam power that operated on these lines took a lot of variety from the American railroading scene. The power of most of these roads was known for its distinctive personality and individualism. Power such as the Southern's sparkling green and gold Pacifics and the Katy's well tended Mikes disappeared along with the Lehigh Valley's singularly distinctive 4-8-4's, and the beautifully toned whistles of the Wabash 4-8-2's and 4-8-4's that so aptly earned the slogan "Wabashing them." The beautifully designed and sturdy Mountains and Northerns of the Missouri Pacific along with all the recently acquired secondhand power of the Chicago & Illinois Midland vanished as did the half a century old 4-6-2's that still wheeled daily the Chicago & Eastern Illinois *Zipper* down the straightaway into St. Louis a scant few minutes ahead of the New York Central's mighty Hudson powered *Southwestern Limited*. True, steam was still pleasurably abundant but for many the romance of the little lines was gone, and many were the pages in the *Official Guide* that no longer held any significance.

The mighty steam empire of the New York Central and the Pennsylvania did not pass unscathed through this period either. Steam lasted another three to four years on both roads but that certain something was missing. The old stand-bys, the familiar faces, were thin and haggard. The banshee wail of the K-4 Pacific had all but disappeared from the standard railroad of the world while on the Empire State Route the world renowned J-3 and J-4 Hudsons were appearing less frequently at the head end of anything but express trains and Cincinnati and Indianapolis division locals. It seems indeed appropriate to regard the passage of these two breeds of steam locomotives as the passage of a race. Every railfan had his favorite breed of steam locomotive and justly so, but what other machines have been so photographed, modeled, and publicized in their life time as the K-4 and J-3?

Nowhere was the essence of speed so apparent in steam motive power as when it sounded in the wail of a K-4's high pitched whistle as it bore down on a small town grade crossing with the *Spirit of St. Louis* across Ohio at a flat 90 an hour; or in the incessant scream atop the gleaming boiler of a New York Central 4-6-4 reeling off the miles on the four-track main west of Cleveland.

One could not think of the motive power of either of these two eastern giants without automatically envisaging either engine, and so although other classes and types remained in service for some time on both lines, the retirement of these two famous types marked the passage of steam on all of the Empire State and Keystone routes.

It is fortunate indeed that the Pennsylvania saw fit, and rightly so, to put on permanent exhibit at Horseshoe Curve K-4 No. 1361 while the New York Central, at last report, has the 5433 preserved in its Harmon, New York enginehouse.

This, then, was the beginning of the end; the experiments were over, the war was over, materials could once again be used in unallocated amounts for the construction of internal-combustion power. The transition from steam to diesel was in full swing. Here on the pages following are the steam locomotives that fell victim during this period in their last days of operation.

Left: The downgrade momentum of 126 freight cars shoving hard at the drawbar of its huge, box car size tender has the Missouri Pacific's big 4-8-4 No. 2213 leaning into a reverse curve near Valley Park, Mo., at close to 65 an hour as it heads west running extra on the St. Louis subdivision of the Eastern division.

The largest locomotives ever to enter Missouri Pacific service weighing in at 231 tons minus tender and equipped with integral cast steel engine beds and roller bearings throughout, the beautifully proportioned 4-8-4's were dual service engines in every sense of the word, performing equally well on a 125 car freight or with 18 heavyweight Pullmans of the *Sunshine Special.*

The 2213 and its fourteen sister engines of this series were built in 1943 by the Baldwin Locomotive Works and according to the war Production Board restrictions in effect at that time patterned after the already existing Denver & Rio Grande Western M-68 class locomotives.

Above: Though its surroundings and operations are as picturesque as it is insolvent, for some reason good action photographs of the Rutland Railroad's light and neatly arranged class L-1 4-8-2's are as rare as their actual numbers. Alco built four of these handsome little Mountain types in 1945, the first new freight power on the system since World War I, and they were immediately swallowed up into the undulating rural countryside of Vermont, seemingly hidden from photographers.

Nevertheless, here is No. 92 smoking through Alfrecha, Vt., with 9 cars of freight RC-2 on its way to North Bennington. When this action was recorded symbol freight RC-2 had been consigned to diesel power for some time and it was only due to the friendly cooperation of Rutland personnel that a change could be effected to enable photographer Sankoff to record the run in steam.

11

Above: Recorded a few months before the ill-fated strike against the railroad in 1953 brought an end to all passenger service on the Rutland, white faced Pacific No. 85 steps smartly out of the railroad's namesake division point at Rutland, Vt., with train No. 87 bound for Alburgh.

Top right: The last of the major New England lines to make the complete switch from steam to diesel, the Central of Vermont kept several of its steam engines active until the late 1950's including a few of its well known 2-10-4's. The venerable Consolidations were the most active during this time.

Central of Vermont No. 466, traces of rust on its boiler flanks, sees one more day of service here as it hustles the way freight to Richford across a rolling meadow near Berkshire, Vt., on May 1st, 1954.

Below, right: Berkshire type No. 9406 of the Pittsburgh & Lake Erie has one of the most unwelcome distinctions of any modern steam locomotive. One of a group of seven class A-2-a 2-8-4's built in 1948 for the P. & L. E. she was the last steam locomotive built by the American Locomotive Company and also the last steam engine built for common carrier use in the United States.

Cursed with the shortest life span of any of the modern steam locomotive designs built in the early and mid-1940s the A-2-a's were ordered by the P. & L. E. to aid in moving a tremendous post war traffic on a railroad already having a reputation as the heaviest tonnage carrier in the country. The shift to diesel power in 1951 put the 9400's on standby service. The 9406 is here moving 78 loads south out of New Castle, Pa., on the Pittsburgh run in September 1953.

These engines bore a marked resemblance to the New York Central System's own celebrated 4-8-4 Niagara class, and were fitted with every modern device.

East, west, north and south, and central too, all had their immortal elements of topography over which the steam giants of our time toiled in tandem and multiple moving a nation's freight. Sherman Hill, Cajon, Saluda, and Cranberry grade all recall pillars of smoke standing straight in the sky as beneath sweating, toiling, fire breathing machines worked with strained motions.

Here on the Delaware and Hudson's eighteen mile long, 960 foot climb from Lanesboro to Ararat, Pa., a graceful limbed "J" class Challenger No. 1507 blackens the summer landscape with coal smoke as her 12 drivers bite into heavily sanded rail, lugging fifty empty company hoppers and 58 miscellaneous loads and empties of time freight RW-4 over the hump at Ararat and down to Carbondale.

Helmstetter's curve is a twisting ribbon of steel laid on a vertical 1.75% climb over the Alleghanies five miles west of Cumberland, Md. Around this near horseshoe bend the steam giants of the Western Maryland Railroad flung themselves in a furious onslaught to move westbound tonnage out of the Potomac River valley and up the Connellsville extension to connections for Pittsburgh. The operating department assigned the biggest it had in steam on this hill and in multiples at that. The biggest, meant its class M-2 4-6-6-4's and class I-2 2-10-0 Decapods.

With sanders wide open to add traction to rails made slippery from rain, two of the biggest are here working all out as the drivers of M-2 No. 1211 grind the sand into a white covering on the rail head while 18 cars to the rear

I-2 No. 1111 replenishes this covering. There are 76 more cars of fast freight WM-3 heeling into the curve behind the Decapod's dripping tank.

The M-2 Challengers of the Western Maryland were the newest and, according to the operating personnel, the worst steam motive power on the system. Their 69" drivers seemed inappropriate for the Alleghany grades and were reportedly rough on the trackwork at high speeds. So the 1200's were the first of the road's modern steam power to be scrapped, the last disappeared in 1952.

Today not only have the M-2's and I-2's gone but even Helmstetter's curve has changed. The bend is now a solitary single track with C.T.C. and the twisting trains are urged onward behind somber black F-7s.

TWO PHOTOS ROBERT MALINOSKI

A monster of the coal pits, Reading 2-8-8-0 No. 1817, class N-1-d, a Baldwin product of 1918, comes tromping across the snow with 19 empty hoppers for the Colonial Colliery at Natalie, Pa., on the day before Christmas in 1951. A fitting present for the lens of photographer Malinoski.

Note the exposed and uninsulated steam inlet pipes to the front cylinders, a veritable plumber's nightmare of elbows, unions, and assorted fittings!

In keeping with the practice of this hard coal hauler the 1817 is built with a Wooten firebox for burning either anthracite coal or its waste product, Culm. Named after General Manager John E. Wooten, who originated the idea, the firebox is placed entirely above the driving wheels providing a much larger grate area than normal. This allowed for a thin fire and a light draft, a necessity for burning this fuel. Wooten fireboxes were not only a trademark of all Reading power but also of its two anthracite hauling cousins, the Central of New Jersey and Delaware & Hudson.

16

Few railroads in the East were as opulent with 4-8-4 Northern type locomotives as was the Lehigh Valley. One of the first rail carriers in the Atlantic states to recognize the need for fast freight service, the route of the Black Diamond invested extensively in these 70″ drivered high speed machines between 1930 and 1940 accumulating five different and distinct classes before all were eventually abandoned in favor of diesel power.

Keeping time with the advertising department's claims, a class T-3 Baldwin product of 1934, No. 5126, is hitting it up through South Plainfield, N. J., on the very eve of steam activity in 1948 with 99 cars of symbol freight SJ-4.

While the term "northern" is generally used to designate the 4-8-4 wheel arrangement the Lehigh Valley preferred to follow the practice of the N.C. & St.L., and N.Y.C. in naming these dual service engines after the territory they traversed and so refers to them as Wyoming types in honor of that part of the Susquehanna Valley which has borne the name since Revolutionary days.

The hogger of the Missouri Pacific's big 4-8-4 No. 2201 is holding the speed to a steady 35 an hour in consideration of an oversize transformer load three cars to the rear. The class N-73 Northern is rolling south over the Chester subdivision of the Illinois division at Bixby, Ill., in January of 1954.

Bumped from their original operating assignments on the hilly divisions between St. Louis and Kansas City, Mo., these large and handsome engines, 15 in all, spent the last year of their existence in operation on this water-level Illinois division of the Mop. Designed primarily to handle tonnage heavy redballs over Missouri's Ozark grades, the 2201 appears completely out of place on this flat, gradeless line. Consolation may be realized, though, since this assignment granted it a reprieve from the torch for fully a year.

With his arm outstretched in greeting, this Missouri Pacific hogger is giving his giant 4-8-2 the reins as he roars up the grade out of Valley Park, Mo., with a seven car Christmas mail extra eastbound at 70 miles an hour.

The 4-8-2 pictured here, No. 5326, is one of seven identical locomotives, numbers 5321 to 5327, rebuilt and modernized by the Mo Pac in 1939 from an earlier design of light U.S.R.A. Mountain type into a most notable example of steam locomotive design. Their modernization included the addition of Baldwin disc drivers, a drop-coupler solid sheet steel pilot, roller bearings on every axle, and the addition of a box car size tender. To their end they wheeled the best of Mo Pac varnish.

Two giants from the Missouri Pacific motive power stables — the helper an ex Wabash 2-10-2 No. 1716, the road engine one of the Mo Pac's heavy 4-8-2's No. 5344 — are fighting the 1.5 percent grade of Kirkwood Hill, Missouri, with a 79 car solid train of coal.

When the summit of the grade is reached at Kirkwood the helper engine will uncouple on the move leaving the big boilered Mountain on its own for the 265 mile run to Kansas City. After taking a fresh tank of water at Kirkwood the Santa Fe helper will drop down the west slope of the hill to assist an eastbound freight to the summit, or with no eastbound drag immediately in view, will run light back to the downtown enginehouse at St. Louis to await the dispatching of another drag on the Hill. This was standard operating practice during the reign of steam on Kirkwood Hill, a doubleheaded 2-10-2 and a robust Mountain or Northern making a thundering run for the grade through the suburbs on the west edge of the city and knuckling down as they hit the grade, stacks exhausting in unison, then offbeat, then together again — a thunderous sight and sound never to be forgotten.

Among railfans, photographers, and the like, and in the publications catering to their interests, the most familiar and popular of the Missouri Pacific's large and varied tribe of steam locomotives were its heavy Mountains and Northern types. While harvesting considerably less in publicity and attention, it was the numerous stock of 2-8-2 Mikados that formed the backbone of the road's freight hauling power; at one time the railroad could boast ownership of 298 such locomotives in varying dimensions and appearances.

By far the largest and most widely used were the 170 engines in the 1400 to 1570 series, a company design based on the U.S.R.A. heavy engine of the same wheel arrangement and, with the exception of headlight placement and sand dome design, quite similar in appearance. Used in the greatest numbers on the Illinois, Kansas, and Arkansas lines of the system, the big Mikes were not to be underestimated when it came to moving tonnage as the 1449 is doing here, over the right of way of the Little Rock division near McGehee, Ark., with 83 cars of a northbound extra thundering behind.

Above: Coupled to a tender whose water capacity would hardly seem adequate to permit the engine to stray out of sight of a water plug, the Missouri Pacific's little tall stacked 4-6-0 No. 2348 waltzes noisily out of Gurdon, Ark., in March 1951 with 23 cars bound for the pulpwood yards along the tracks between Gurdon and Norman, Ark., listed in the employees' operating timecard somewhat dubiously as the "Delight subdivision."

For fully a year and a half after the Mo Pac had proudly anounced *complete* dieselization of its entire system, the 2348 and two identical engines continued their daily trips to Norman and back, because the weight restrictions on several timber bridges, which are quite numerous the whole length of the Delight subdivision, were too low to permit use of any standard diesel motive power unit.

Needless to say, the movements of the 2348 and her two sisters were kept top secret during this time.

At right: A true Mallet Compound of the World War I Railroad Administration, the Virginian's 2-8-8-2 No. 722 articulates boldly around a curve deep in a wooded valley midway between Page and Deepwater, W. Va., with several empty refrigerator and box cars and interspersed with loaded hoppers for interchange with the New York Central at Dickinson.

Picking its way through the smoke and haze that lay perpetually over the rail yard blanketed river bottoms of the East St. Louis, Ill., rail terminal in days of steam, the New York Central's 4-8-2 No. 2917 seeks its own receiving yards with a westbound Big Four Route manifest. Though the engine itself has crested the hump that leads into the yard, it is still working steam since the majority of its 73 car train hangs over the summit on the ascending grade.

New York Central Mohawk No. 3000, a smoke deflectored 4-8-2, is wheeling the mail as it roars through the
early morning congestion at Englewood station in south
Chicago, Ill., with a 10 car mail and express extra east.

Laboring heavily on a short but steep grade near Deepwater, W. Va., the Virginian's aged 2-8-8-2 Mallet No. 710
is bringing a 147 car train of coal up the New York Central's Kanawha branch into the Dickinson yards at Charles-
ton for interchange with that road.

The Virginian enjoys trackage rights of the Central's
Kanawha branch from the Deepwater crossing of the Kanawha River to the Dickinson yards, and it is this connection
that gives the New York Central a competitive position
for the Pocahontas coal traffic.

The New York Central's No. 407, the *Cleveland-St. Louis Special,* with 13 cars of mail and express rolls past the home signals guarding the junction with the Gulf, Mobile & Ohio's main line at Mitchell, Ill. The 79 inch drivered 4-6-2 on the head end, No. 4915, still retains the disc drivers, and semi streamlined cab with which it was equipped while assigned to the Chicago-Detroit *Mercury* run in 1936. Its driving wheels illuminated at night and shrouded in a streamline, sheet metal cowling that more nearly resembled an overturned bathtub, the engine and train were the talk of the railroad world. Crossings were specially guarded because of its deceptive speed.

The advent of the famous streamlined Hudsons and their assignment to this train brought about the removal of the 4915's streamlining and wheel illumination, leaving it fit for less spectacular hauls. It and a sister engine, No. 4917, which also went through this phase, rolled out their miles on the Big Four Route's rails.

The 12 cars of the New York Central's *Carolina Special* have rolled the 55 miles from Chicago to Kankakee, Ill., behind a square domed Illinois Central 4-8-2 in accordance with the standard procedure used by the two railroads in handling Chicago-Cincinnati passenger trains of the Central. At Kankakee, however, a more customary New York Central Hudson was dispatched from the enginehouse there and is now accelerating the mixed heavy and lightweight equipment of the train southward on the Central's own rails.

Below: For some time after diesel power had bumped steam from the main line of the Kansas City Southern, 2-10-2 No. 220 performed daily hauling of empties south and loads north on the Baxter Springs branch serving the strip coal mines near that Oklahoma community.

Though the K.C.S. did originate 10 of its own self styled 2-10-4's, the several 2-10-2's it owned were all acquired secondhand from the Wabash and like No. 220 and its three sister engines, the 221 to 223, from the Ann Arbor.

The light U.S.R.A. 2-10-2 is here raising hob with the Sunday evening quiet at Pittsburgh, Kan., as it exhausts heavily across the town's main street with 83 cars of strip coal behind its auxiliary water tender as it heads for the classification yards north of town.

The 220's trip thru town will take it past the K.C.S.'s huge, once bustling steam locomotive repair shops, one of the largest in the southwest where its exhaust will fade away among the now abandoned rows of denuded boilers and frames awaiting the repairs that will never come.

At right: On the little known Eastern Illinois division of the New York Central System a class H-10b 2-8-2 No. 2090 tromps over the Baltimore & Ohio's diamond at Norris City, Ill. The 92 cars of assorted freight lumbering behind are being pelted by a hail of cinders from the hard working Mike.

The Eastern Illinois division drops like a tentacle from the main line near Chicago and reaches all the way into the southern Illinois coal fields near Harrisburg, finally terminating in a small three stall enginehouse located at the very tip of the state at Cairo at the confluence of the mighty Mississippi and Ohio rivers just beyond track's end.

The line at one time boasted of its own overnight passenger haul. Designated as Nos. 463 and 464, the *Egyptian* after the territory it served, the four car local is shown here behind Pacific No. 4909 at Norris City, Ill., shortly after dawn on the southward haul.

Above: Fresh from the back shops at Jackson, Ohio, the Detroit, Toledo & Ironton's Lima built 2-8-2 No. 811 thunders up the grade into Springfield, Ohio, with 55 cars of northbound symbol freight DT-2.

At the Springfield Terminal the 811 will be serviced in an enginehouse modern enough to bring envy into the hearts of every La Grange designer. A fluorescent lighted, three track, through type brick structure with the latest in servicing equipment, it was refreshing to find a railroad that believed modern steam power deserved modern facilities.

By 1955 the tracks to this modern facility had been taken up and the building sold to a private industrial firm, while on the nearby main iron the flaming vermillion GP-9's of the newly dieselized D. T. & I. rolled by with hardly a glance at the Springfield Yard.

Top, right: Prior to its abandonment in 1952, the only direct rail passenger service between Louisville and St. Louis was this abbreviated consist of two head end cars and one coach operated on a leisurely nine hour schedule by the Southern Railway.

The scrapping of the little train, brought about by the Post Office Department's decision to replace short haul R.P.O. service with trucks, spelled the end of passenger service on the Southern's St. Louis division.

It also meant the end for four of the Southern's little green and gold painted 4-6-2's, the 1231, 1234, 1317, and 1324. All were class PS-2 engines, beautifully painted and maintained to the last, such as the 1317 here wheeling the eastbound counterpart of this varnish haul, No. 24, around a curve near Belleville, Ill. Built by Richmond in 1906, they remained in service for some time after their more famous offspring, the class PS-4 Pacifics, had been relegated to the scrap yard.

Below, right: Running on the left hand main, as is standard Chicago & Northwestern operating practice, a fat-boilered class H 4-8-4 No. 3027 surges up a slight sag with 78 cars of time freight No. 124 at Villa Park, Ill.

The class H Northerns are one of the earlier designs of 4-8-4's, built in 1929 by Baldwin Locomotive Works. Though originally constructed with 76 inch spoke drivers and outside journal lead trucks, the 30 engines of this series carried a note of modernity in their all welded tanks and high horsepower. The engines' appearance was changed considerably in 1946 by the addition of Box Pok drivers and a huge rotating "Mars" light.

Like true 4-8-4's, they made time across the undulating trackage of the Galena division with mail trains and refrigerator drags alike. A famous breed of engine on a famous road.

Above: Its tender bearing the insignia of the Chicago & Northwestern while its cab carries the initials of its leased parent road, a U.S.R.A. heavy Mikado No. 424 of the Chicago, St. Paul, Minneapolis & Omaha is rolling across the Wisconsin dairyland near Chippewa Falls. Its train of 98 cars is headed south on the single track Duluth to Eau Claire line in the summer of 1953.

Top right: At Nelson, Ill., under an array of the horizontally mounted block signals peculiar to the Chicago & Northwestern, a class E-4 streamlined Hudson No. 4002, its olive green shrouding the worse for wear and inattention, is hurrying east at 70 an hour with 12 cars of mail and express. Only the day before, this consist descended the slopes of Sherman Hill, Wyo., behind a smoke deflectored Union Pacific 4-8-4.

Below, right: With the *City of Denver* following close on its markers, the Chicago & Northwestern's Box Pok drivered Pacific No. 1648, its exhaust turning white in the near zero early morning air, is scurrying through Villa Park, Ill., with six cars of Clinton, Iowa, to Chicago overnight local No. 26.

By fall of 1952 the Chicago, Rock Island & Pacific had committed itself to complete dieselization and was steadily advancing toward "D" Day, but like so many of its midwestern neighbors who had ordered newly designed steam locomotives during the Second World War it found itself with a fleet of 20 modern 4-8-4's, newly built in 1944 and 1946, that had not fully paid for themselves in terms of mileage. This condition could not exist and so, to keep the auditors in a happy state of mind, the big Northerns were taken from mediocre assignments and dead lines and put to work with a vengeance.

The Chicago division, extending as far as Silvis Yard at Rock Island, Ill., where for two years previous a steam engine was an oddity, echoed once again to the thunderous exhausts of steam as the big 4-8-4's rolled manifest freight and drag alike, the only discordant note of dieselization occurring with the passage of the transcontinental *Rockets* and the *Golden State*. Turnarounds at the engine terminals were performed with a minimum amount of time, the engines being kept on the road as much as possible.

The autumn months of October and November in northern Illinois were pleasant with the early morning frost, the trees in fall dress, and the chant of big steam power working the long grade out of the Illinois River valley at Joliet, just as No. 5117 is doing with 52 cars of redball tonnage after a stop at Joliet to cross over to the east main to let a Chicago bound *Rocket* streamliner run around it.

The 5117 is in action again at left, this time double-headed with the 5114 dropping down the long grade through Lenox, Ill., at 60 an hour with a 100 car westbound *Rocket* time freight whose consist includes a dead "A" unit diesel coupled behind the 5114's giant tender.

With the approach of winter, however, the deed was done. Practically all of the 5100 class Northerns ended their last run at Blue Island Yard in Chicago where their fires were killed. They were hauled unceremoniously away to a storage track to await their eventual doom. The biggest of steam on the Rock Island Line was dead but not without a last fling at the glorious life it had led.

Above: Of the many soul satisfying sounds emitted from the steam locomotive certainly the sound of its whistle will be the most cherished and remembered. The lonesome, spine tingling wail of this most beautiful of sounds as it floated across a darkened landscape on a quiet summer's night is not easily nor soon forgotten.

Though it was crime enough for the diesel with its air horn to still this most beautiful of sounds, it was even more deceitful for a steam locomotive to be denied the ability to create this magic music while yet alive. Such was the case with those beautiful red and orange GS-4 Daylight engines of the Southern Pacific, the mighty Niagaras of the New York Central, and both Hudsons and Northerns of the Milwaukee Road.

These engines were equipped with an air horn whose monotoned voice was enough to bring shame to their head end crews.

Despite its heavy exhaust and handsome design the air horn mounted atop the smokebox of the Milwaukee Road's 4-8-4 No. 215 strikes a note of discord as it blares loudly for the several grade crossings ahead while the S-2 class Northern walks a 36 car extra west out of the Bensenville Yards.

At right: Heading a solid train of eastbound perishables, the Northern Pacific's class A-5 Northern type No. 2682 prepares to take on coal at the Sartell, Minn., coal chute. On the adjacent track Mikado No. 1806, exhausts rapidly in an effort to pull ahead.

A few miles north of Little Falls, Minn. the Northern Pacific's No. 2677, a 77 inch drivered Northern eases 142 cars of livestock and perishables east out onto the main line. The 2677 is equipped with the pressed steel type pilot that seemingly found favor only on the Northern Pacific and its affiliate, the Burlington.

The N.P., for which the 4-8-4 Northern type was named since that road was first to use such a wheel arrangement, had at one time six separate classes of 4-8-4's. A total of 49 engines, they were, with the exception of tender design

and weights, similar in over-all design and driving wheel size. All had that unmistakable N.P. trademark, the large, flat lensed headlight.

Without a doubt the most notable of this tribe was the 2626, the original Timken Roller Bearing equipped engine No. 1111, which performed in exhaustive tests on railroads throughout the United States to extol the virtues of roller bearing equipped motive power. Purchased from Timken by the N.P. in 1933, this engine performed continuously and creditably until its retirement as recently as early 1959.

Below: Working with throttle in the corner one of the Northern Pacific's fearsome looking Z-5 class, No. 5120, comes charging out of the yards at Livingston, Montana, ready to do battle with the 1.5% ascending grade of Bozeman Pass.

The 5120 is not alone in its battle, though. 108 cars to the rear, one of the N.P.'s famous 2-8-8-4 Yellowstones, No. 5005, shoves hard against the steel crummy to keep the slack bunched. On the date of this action in July 1954 the 5005 was one of three of the original 10 Yellowstones still in service.

It is questionable whether more rail fans have journeyed to Duluth, Minn., to witness the heavy tonage operations of the mighty U.S. Steel owned Duluth, Missabe & Iron Range or to view with fascination and feeling the home-spun, quaint doings of the Duluth, Winnipeg & Pacific. A wholly owned subsidiary of the Canadian National, the 170 mile long D. W. & P. leaves its parent rails at Fort Frances, Ontario, and heads in as straight a line as the topography will permit for the shores of Lake Superior.

Its antique, orange painted, frame enginehouse perched on a rocky outcrop above the bay was haven to a family of sturdy 2-8-0's whose stronghold was challenged only once daily by the 4-6-2 Pacific used on the lone passenger haul. The stout Consolidations were used in twos and threes to pull and push the 30 to 40 car consists of north-bound freights up the hill from the lake front.

One of these daily freight hauls of 37 cars is shown behind one of the 2-8-0's, this one, No. 2460, fitted with a Coffin feedwater heater hung ahead of the smokebox door and a fireboy who appears to be well at ease in the cab window.

The lone pasenger haul over the single track iron of the D. W. & P. is shown rolling downgrade into the city limits of Duluth on a quiet Sunday morning in June 1953 behind a neatly proportioned 4-6-2 No. 5098 of the parent Canadian National, the D. W. & P. itself not being pos-sessed of any passenger motive power.

Missouri-Kansas-Texas graphite faced Pacific No. 396 urges the 12 heavy standard weight Pullmans, coaches, and head end cars of the St. Louis bound *Katy Flyer* into motion after a stop for water at St. Charles, Mo.

The generous amount of white trim on running boards and wheel rims topped off by the large *Katy* herald in red and white on the tender flanks was for years a trademark of the neat and immaculately maintained steam motive power of M-K-T, which until the advent of the diesel rolled its freight and passengers behind steam power no larger than a 2-8-2 or 4-6-2 of the type pictured above.

41

Noted for its fast carded Blue Streak freight schedules, its photogenic engines and their melodious whistles in the night, the St. Louis-Southwestern operated its 20 handsome, high wheeling 4-8-4's into the very eve of dieselization. These 70 inch drivered machines set daily records with symbol freights and California perishable blocks alike as they romped across the Arkansas ricelands and Mississippi River bottoms in their race with time and competition from the paralleling and in one instance the joint rails of such larger giants as the Missouri Pacific and Illinois Central.

Although for years the Cotton Belt hauled its freight almost totally with a fleet of World War I 2-8-0's, unlike so many midwestern railroads it never purchased or operated a 2-8-2 Mikado. Instead, when the need for faster scheduling of freight became apparent in the 1920's, the road bypassed the 2-8-2, a natural offshoot of the 2-8-0, and immediately ordered the first ten of these notable North-erns from the Baldwin Locomotive Works in 1930, following up with 10 more from its own shops at Pine Bluff, Ark., in 1937.

This author will never forget the lonely little depot at Brainard, Ark., on a bright, moonlit night with the click of the wireless the only sound to break the stillness, while far to the south the headlight of the 819 bored steadily onward with symbol freight IV-10 rolling behind. The engine's melodious whistle in the night brought the sleepy-eyed agent out on the platform to wave a highball. It sighed and mournfully disappeared into the clear night air.

In the view below the 819 returns to the right hand iron as it rolls off the five mile stretch of Centralized Traffic Control track between the East St. Louis yards and Dupo, Ill., whipping through the high speed crossovers at North Dupo tower with a southbound extra of overflow manifest freight.

The Pensylvania's mighty class T-1 duplex-drive 4-4-4-4 No. 5500 is reeling off the Illinois miles as it races east at Washington Park at 80 miles an hour with 14 cars of No. 64, the now discontinued, all coach *Jeffersonian*. The most striking and individualistic of all Pennsylvania passenger locomotives, 52 T-1's were built between 1942 and 1946 by both Baldwin Locomotive Works and the Pennsy's own Altoona shops. Designed to handle with ease an 880 ton passenger train at 100 miles an hour on level, tangent track, they outperformed a 5400 horse-power diesel at all speeds above 20 miles an hour. Despite this acclaim and numerous superlatives tacked onto them, the T-1's were an unhappy experience for the Pennsylvania. Excessive maintenance costs of the Poppet valve system and slippery footing, especially so in the forward unit, were the chief cause for complaint. A K-4s 4-6-2 with some 20,000 less pounds of tractive effort could start an almost identical weight train easier than could a T-1. Ironically enough, scores of the system's 1924 and 1927 built K-4s Pacifics worked in main line passenger service for

some three to four years after the T-1's were stored away at Altoona. A notable design nonetheless, the T-1's appeared at an unfortunate time. The duplex-drive never reached maturity.

There is one school of thought among students of steam power that the Pennsylvania would not have been so eager to dieselize had it invested in a more conventional 4-8-4 based on a design similar to that of the Santa Fe or Union Pacific. A matter for conjecture.

It is interesting to note the Pennsylvania, often heralded as the standard setting railroad of the world, once pridefully disdaining the mechanical designs and practices of the rest of the railroad industry for the accomplishments of its own designers and craftsmen who justifiably turned out some of the most distinctly different and successful steam engines in the country, now accepts and adheres closely, with all others, to that most mass produced of motive power designs, the diesel electric. No matter for conjecture here, a simple matter of economics.

As full dieselization became imminent, many were the roads that cheerfully stored away their remaining steam power on little-used rails to rust and deteriorate with the seasons. Yet when an abnormally high traffic movement unexpectedly occurred, it was to these graveyards of steam power they turned for aid. The photographer was informed by the Altoona enginehouse force that only the day before, this rust covered Mountain type of the Pennsylvania Railroad, M-1a No. 6861, had been pulled from the ranks of the dead, revived with life-giving steam, and put to moving tonnage over the Altoona-Enola district. Showing plenty of life yet, it was hitting a good 45 an hour as it leaned into the curve at Lewistown, Pa., with 140 cars, the majority coal laden hoppers, stretched out behind its tank. Seconds after this photograph was taken,

the engine's 72 inch drivers lost their grip on the well polished curve and spun wildly until the hogger shoved in the throttle a notch or two, whereupon the big Mountain regained its slippery footing and thundered on.

Just as the K-4 Pacific was the classic passenger locomotive of the Pennsylvania so the M-1 4-8-2 was the freight counterpart. Over 300 engines of this wheel arrangement finally saw service over all the steam powered main line divisions. Designed by the Altoona Works of the Pennsy itself in 1923 this group of locomotives was given justifiable praise, albiet reluctantly, for in times of motive power scarcity just prior to full dieselization they were called upon again and again, just as pictured above, to relieve the traffic congestion on the system's all important eastern divisions.

Bearing the brunt of the enormous World War II traffic and caught without any really new or completely modern freight locomotives for its non-electrified territory, the Pennsylvania in 1943 broke tradition and turned to a completely new, to the Pennsy, wheel arrangement. War Production Board regulations and a premium on time prevented the usual experimentation and custom design. The road finally adopted the design of the T-1 class 2-10-4 of the Chesapeake and Ohio, an eminently successful engine. Generally and officially conceded to be one of the finest steam locomotives to bear the famous keystone number plate, the system finally wound up with 127 such machines. Visible modifications from the C. & O. prototype were the all welded 16 wheel tanks, a streamlined cab, a front end arrangement more in keeping with the Pennsylvania practice, and a massive, consolidated sand and steam dome.

Used most extensively on lines west of Crestline, Ohio, the J-1 class, as they were designated, appeared in later years on Horseshoe Curve, their last service before retirement being in the form of helper engines on the famous grade out of Altoona, Pa.

In happier days before this semi and permanent retirement, J-1a No. 6171, after a brief wait for the *Spirit of St. Louis* to pass, roars out of the East St. Louis, Ill., yards and through the crossovers of "HN" Cabin, interlocking with 99 cars of time freight SL-2 rumbling behind.

Shown here are two more Pennsylvania Railroad M-1a class Mountains revitalized for service during the traffic upsurge of 1955-56. Not so healthy, though, are these two, the effects of long inaction on the Altoona storage tracks having had their ill effects. Lead engine No. 6907 has been deadheaded over light from Altoona to Lewistown to await the arrival of the 6704 and its westbound drag of 103 cars. Halfway between Enola yards and Lewistown, the 6704's stoker mechanism took sick and refused to function. In order to keep moving, the head end crew resorted to hand firing, a task near torture in the cab heat on a hot July day. The 6907 was itself somewhat of an invalid. Besides developing a hot tank journal on the way over from Altoona, its stack was a rusty remnant leaking smoke from a myriad of holes. Its most noticeable sign of deterioration was the absence of the proud Keystone number plate on its smokebox door. Some enginehouse employee had painted the engine number in large, staggered digits over the accustomed location.

With the air pumped up and the fireboy on the 6704 heaving a sigh of relief, the invalids staggered out of town. The sound of their going belied their ailments.

Above: Brought out of storage in the dead line at the Decatur yards to help in moving a bumper crop of soy beans, Wabash 4-8-4 No. 2916 is enjoying a brief reprieve from the scrap torch in February of 1952.

Here under the girders of the Illinois Terminal's overpass at Mitchell, Ill., the hogger is sanding the rails as he works with the throttle in the corner to urge 53 loaded box cars into motion.

Right, top: Running some three hours late, the Pennsylvania's 14 car No. 65, the *Jeffersonian,* pounds across the Louisville and Nashville's diamond at "Q" tower in East St. Louis, Ill. East of Indianapolis the second unit of its Baldwin built, centipede truck diesel went lame. Emergency aid being of no avail, the single functioning unit limped into Terre Haute where K-4 No. 5482 was coupled to the head end. The 4-6-2 had been on standby duty at that terminal. With the combined tractive effort of the diesel and the speed of the famous 80 inch drivered Pa-

cific at hand, the team lost little time covering the 160 miles across the Illinois division.

Right, bottom: In the days of steam operations the greatest identifying characteristic of any railroad was its motive power. One need only mention a company name and the process of imagination immediately conjured up a vision of one's favorite model or the most publicized engine of that road. Rarely, though, have two names been as synonymous as that of the Pennsylvania and its classic K-4s Pacific design. For years the favorite prototype of modelers and certainly the world's most publicized locomotive, the K-4s was a trademark in steam for the mighty Pennsy. It is justifiably fitting that the K-4s be among the last of steam. Their once legendary numbers, some 425, were reduced to a handful by the early 1950's.

Here on the Logansport division at Dwyer, Ind., in 1952, a remnant of this once proud fleet, is about to hammer away at the Grand Trunk Western's diamond with eastbound passenger No. 117.

Left, top: The year is 1954 and the Wabash Railway has been completely dieselized for some two years. Here on Wabash rails, however, an 1899 vintage F-4 class Mogul No. 573 shuffles past the order board at Clayton, Ill., with five cars of the daily freight run over the Bluffs, Ill., to Keokuk, Iowa branch.

The longevity of steam power on this branch may be credited to a seven span swing bridge across the Illinois River at Meredosia, whose aged and spindly beams will support nothing heavier than a 2-6-0, and one at a time if you please!

While GP-7's set out the tonange at the Bluffs yards, it remained for the Johnson bar-equipped old-timers like No. 573 here to baby the consists across the weight restrictive bridge.

The management in late 1954 quietly and determinedly put an end to these shenanigans by installing two leased Pennsylvania Railroad 44 ton G.E. diesel switchers, and thus brought to an end 50 odd years of Mogulism on the Keokuk Line.

Left, bottom: There are 59 cars of L.C.L. merchandise and auto parts destined for the assembly lines at St. Louis churning the dust from the roadbed as they whip across the Alton & Southern's diamond at Mitchell, Ill., at 70 miles an hour behind Wabash 4-8-2 No. 2823. The train is Acme Fast Freight No. 89, and for it to lag a minute behind schedule raises the eyebrows under brass hats the length of the division, so the hoghead on this particular day is really "Wabashing" the high cars.

Below: Long since removed from its once plushier assignments on the head end of the Blue Bird and Banner Blue varnish runs, Wabash Hudson No. 706 must accept insult on injury by asissting a three unit E.M.D. product in moving a drag freight up the long grade out of the Illinois River valley at Bluffs, Ill.

The two locomotives are operating on the Wabash Decatur, Ill., to Moberly, Mo., line which forms an essential link in the road's east-west through service.

Above: Secondhand power was a prevalent item on the Chicago & Illinois Midland. The road owned at one time or another locomotives from the Burlington, Pittsburgh & Lake Erie, Big Four Route, Lackawanna, Wabash, and its latest purchases in 1952 from the Atlantic Coast Line, nine 2000 class 2-10-2's.

By far the investment which paid off most were nine ex Wabash Santa Fe types of that road's 2500 class. These World War I vintage products of Alco served continuously and faithfully in both mine switching and road haul work until the retirement of all steam in 1955.

Sporting a newly acquired tender, a castoff from a scrapped New York Central L-1, this truly mongrel breed of engine, ex Wabash No. 2518, now C. & I. M. No. 655, has just finished doubling the 1% hill between Petersburg and Hill Top.

Right: The Chicago & Illinois Midland is roughly 125 miles of beautifully maintained right of way over which rolls a steady stream of enormous coal filled gondolas from the mines south of Springfield, Ill., to the car dumper at Havana, Ill. In days of steam, there also rolled over this beautiful trackage some of the best maintained locomotives in the kingdom of steam.

C. & I. M. steam power was for the most part ten-coupled U.S.R.A. in design with its inherent balanced wheel spacing, beautifully tapered boilers, and balanced cab size. The addition of Delta trailing trucks, and in later years longer tanks acquired from the New York Central off scrapped 4-8-2 Mohawks, only served to better this design.

All this is immediately evident in U.S.R.A. 2-10-2 No. 700, thundering across a branch of the Sangamon River near Kilbourne, Ill., with 71 empty hoppers just off the car dumper at Havana. The red striped tank and green and gold heraldry on its side are proud trademarks of the road's motive power department.

Another U.S.R.A. design, No. 701, repeats the process, only this time on the Sangamon River bridge itself with an even 100 empties.

At Leithton, Ill., the Soo Line's 4-8-4 No. 5003 has taken slack twice in attempting to start a northward extra of 68 cars. The big Northern has stopped to set out a car at the Chicago, North Shore & Milwaukee interchange track, leaving the remainder of its train sitting in a steep sided sag. It took a considerable amount of urging from the hoghead coupled with a generous use of the sanders before more level terrain was reached.

The 5003 is one of four Northern types built for the Soo in 1938 by Lima Locomotive Works, becoming the road's heaviest and most modern steam power.

Black and shining in the early morning sun, the Chicago & Illinois Midland's No. 502, which with its sister engines, the 500 and 501, were the last 4-4-0 American type locomotives built for commercial use in the United States (the year 1927 being their birthdate) smokes out of Springfield, Ill., on a summer's day in 1951 on the Springfield to Pekin passenger haul.

The highball signal under which the 502 is passing will never move to halt a C. & I. M. train since it guards the crossing of the Springfield Terminal Railroad, long since a defunct and non-operating property at the time of this exposure. Today both the signal and the train are gone, the short lived 4-4-0's reduced to scrap and the C. & I. M. a freight only line.

In typical three-quarter pose the Great Northern's 2-10-2 No. 2186 rolls grandly south near Breckenridge, Minn., under an impressive canopy of steam made distinct in the early morning near zero temperature.

The 2186 is one of nearly four score such steamers returned to service along with mallet 2053 during the summer of 1956 providing a lasting impression of the heaviest in steam on the Empire Builder route.

Great Northern

The motive power stables of the Great Northern have been the between-assignments resting place for a host of true Mallet articulated power since the turn of the century. Their wheel classification ranged from stubby boilered 2-6-6-2's and enormous 2-8-8-0's to the 2-6-8-0 oddities used on the Mesabi iron range. The various designs all shared a monstrous, almost fiendish look, due in part to the large boilers and generous amount of plumbing hung on the front end. This tremendous array of iron and steel adorning the smokebox end was enough to scare even the nerviest motorist who dared race one of these fearsome beasts to a grade crossing.

By the summer of 1956 the inroads of diesel power had eliminated this herd of steam giants to such an extent that on all the far-flung rails of the big "G" only one Mallet was to be found in operation. This was the 2053, a class R-2 2-8-8-2, the biggest and heaviest the Great Northern ever owned. Confined to the division between Grand Forks and Devils Lake, North Dakota, it was a constant source of irritation to the enginehouse foremen at both division pionts. What with its operating parts in such a state of neglect it was constantly in need of repairs and excess attention. Consequently each enginehouse force would do only what was absolutely necessary to get it on the road again in the hope it would not return for some time.

Luck was lacking for the enginehouse force at Grand Forks on this date, however, as the big Mallet headed east with 145 cars of grain and lumber tied to its big Vanderbilt tank. Its coming had been announced for fully twenty minutes by a tall pillar of oil smoke towering over the flat Dakota prairie, punctuated by the thundering roll of its exhaust. Sporting a flat-top haircut, the youngish looking hoghead at her controls seemed oblivious to any mechanical defects as he thundered down the thirty-mile stretch of tangent iron between Larimore and Grand Forks under a tremendous canopy of black smoke at earth shaking speeds of up to 50 an hour. The big bruiser was rocking and rolling so from this headlong lunge it appeared as though at any moment she would leap from the rails and take to the adjoining fields. She rolled grandly and smokily into the yards at Grand Forks without incident, though, no doubt to the dismay of the enginehouse crew which had dispatched her west only the night before with the hope she would not return.

By way of tribute to the 2053's staunch determination to stay alive and running during this reprieve a mention of other records attributable to her and 16 sister class R-2s might be of interest. Although U.P.'s Big Boys were heavier no other simple articulated could equal the mountain leveling 147,000 pound tractive effort of the R-2s. A product of the G.N.'s own Hillyard, Washington shops in 1927 they were the first steam locomotives built west of the Mississippi River and also the largest power built with a Belpaire boiler. Tipping the scales at close to 530 tons each these engines could also claim a distinction of being, at one time, the most colorful articulated in steam, since their original livery called for the traditional G.N. deep sea green on the boiler jacket and cylinder lagging. Unfortunately, this colorful practice was dropped with the advent of diesel power and the 2053 finished out her days in the accustomed locomotive black.

Above and at left: Two pictures of No. 2053, the biggest and heaviest giant the Great Northern ever owned. By the summer of 1956 this was the last Mallet in operation on the big "G."

Whether perpetrated in anguish at drawing a smoke belching steamer instead of a more plushy diesel, or due to pride at being chosen to handle the last and biggest on the road the close cropped hoghead at the throttle was working steam with a vengeance, definitely pleasing to the photographer, if not to the operating department.

The abundant grain harvest in 1956 brought additional steam power out of storage on the Great Northern beside the previously mentioned Mallet No. 2053. With the beginning movement of grain to market the eastern division points blossomed forth in steam. Grand Forks, Fargo, Breckenridge, and even the Minneapolis enginehouse once again housed hot and smoking Mikes and Mountains. The diesels had been called west to bolster motive power forces on divisions already given to dieselization where all steam facilities had been removed. It was a field day for steam and for the photographer lucky enough to be there.

In the view above, 4-8-2 No. 2525 winds through a stand of trees near Avon, Minn., with 76 cars of northbound freight.

At the top of the page opposite, one of the big "G's" tremendously large class 0-8 2-8-2's No. 3388, built in the company shops with 69 inch driving wheels making it the highest drivered Mikado ever built, is roaring across the North Dakota prairie near Buxton at 50 an hour with 109 empty box cars destined for lumber loading in the Northwest.

Beneath it the 2551, a 4-8-4 with driving wheels not much larger, 72 inches to be exact, pulls through the passing track at Larimore, N. D., after meeting an eastbound local passenger in the form of a self-propelled coach-baggage unit. The 2551 is running extra with 83 cars on the Grand Forks to Devils Lake district.

On a June morning in 1956 the 1753 and 4345 are making the hills resound with stack talk as they roll over a cinder ballasted right of way laid on tailings and tipple waste washed into the Shamokin Creek valley from long abandoned mines. A mile distant at Crowl, a seemingly uninhabited hamlet with a passing track and a general store to testify to its existence, another pair of I-1's are waiting to couple on and shove at the hind end of the 88 car consist. These two helpers had labored on the rear of an earlier dispatched ore drag to Mt. Carmel and have drifted back downgrade to await the 1753's and 4345's arrival, their crews relaxing meanwhile in the antique atmosphere of Crowl's lone business establishment.

Ore for the Mills of Bethlehem

In the light of such notables as Horseshoe Curve, multiple track right of way, and its legendary K-4 locomotives, the Pennsylvania's little known 27-mile long branch line between Northumberland and Mt. Carmel, Pa., would seem to be of little significance. Yet in view of its length, its cinder ballasted roadbed, and the small type announcing its existence in the *Official Guide,* it sees the passage of more locomotives and tonnage than any comparable branch line in the United States. This claim for notoriety stems from its existence as a link in the shortest rail route for moving Minnesota and foreign mined iron ore from the Great Lakes docks at Erie, Pa., to the Bethlehem Steel mills at Bethlehem, Pa. This ore moves in standard tonnage hoppers over the rails of the Pennsylvania's Susquehanna division to arrive eventually in the yards at Northumberland to await the final and most dramatic part of its trip.

For although a single M-1a 4-8-2 steam engine may wheel a 9000-ton train of ore down the water level, gradeless Susquehanna division without effort, it requires no less than four of the Pennsy's powerful I-1 class 2-10-0 Decapods to move the same train the 27 miles to Mt. Carmel. Although the line may lack length, it apologizes for the deficiency with a tortuous 1.3% grade on the final 8½ miles between Shamokin and Mt. Carmel. Combine these ingredients of tonnage and grades with heavy steam power and the inevitable occurs, an operating department's headache and a railfan's delight.

The great bulk of the Shamokin branch ore tonnage was handled by the Pennsy's famous hippo shaped I-1 Decapods since the seasonal tonnage and low mileage made for a very judicious use of steam power at a time when engine dispatchers hesitated to confine a costly diesel to such a short haul. An ironic note worthy of mention here is that in November of 1956, when all the highly touted duplex drive T-1's and Q-2's on which the Pennsylvania had pinned its hopes of continuing with coal fired motive power were either scrapped or rusting away on a forgotten Altoona siding, there remained 113 of the original 582 1923-built I-1's on active service all over the system.

By far the best location for observing these behemoths in action was the Shamokin branch, for here the heavy boilered engines ruled supreme. Their hold on the Shamokin was threatened more than once by internal combustion power, either on test runs or when too many of the I-1's were ill in the shops, an occurrence all too common when enginehouse forces were reluctant to perform any costly repairs to steam power in the face of anticipated dieselization.

But the summers of 1955 and 1956 found the I-1's firmly entrenched, and marching thunderously through Shamokin Creek valley shoulder to shoulder as they kept the red stained hoppers moving east. During this time five to six trains a day of ore were boosted up this hill, each averaging 9000 tons and involving no less than 12 to 16 different Decapods in their movement.

Dawn on any summer's day in 1955 found a half dozen or more squat drivered I-1's emerging from the enginehouse at Northumberland. They moved in groups of two into the dew dampened yards alongside the long trains of red stained hoppers classified during the night and now ready for the final boost to the open hearth. Once having selected their train, they moved in and coupled on, a pair fore and aft. At a signal from the lead engine, pushing and pulling, the four engines moved ponderously out onto the Susquehanna River bridge, past the tower at Sunbury, and out onto the Shamokin Creek valley. The first few miles of the line follow this valley floor allowing the hoggers to work up momentum for the steeper climb ahead. By the time the train rolls through the coal mining community of Paxinos, all four Decapods are down on their hands and knees. When the summit is reached at Mt. Carmel, the train is turned over to the Lehigh Valley for forwarding to Bethlehem. The 2-10-0's pick up their caboose and drift back downgrade to gird for battle once again.

Four hefty voiced 2-10-0's are speaking in unison here as the 4241 and 4554 and two pushers swing into action on the Northumberland bridge.

The second engine hidden from view on the sharp curvature, the 4241 and 4511 are slugging hard as they bend to the 13.9 degree curve at Shamokin with 97 cars of Mesabi rust dragging behind. The high level trackage in the background is the Reading's branch into Shamokin.

Bright and shining from a vigorous rubdown by the roundhouse force, one of the Frisco's fleet of Pacific types, this one No. 1044, equipped with a combination sheet metal and slat type pilot designed to prevent derailments during collisions with cattle, vehicles, and the like, exhausts sharply on the upgrade through Shrewsbury, Mo., on the head end of the Memphis bound *Sunnyland*.

These little 4-6-2's were well known by admirers of Frisco motive power for their sharp, staccato exhaust and with relatively low 69 inch driving wheels for a Pacific type, the passage of one of these engines on a steep upgrade was indeed a sound to stir the senses.

The Frisco's Spit and Polish

There were few roads in the United States that exercised more diligent care and maintenance on their steam motive power than did the St. Louis-San Francisco Lines. This was evident in the gleaming boiler jackets, gold striped tenders and domes, silvered cylinder heads, and red painted number plates.

It is to the Frisco's credit that even during the pressing days of World War II, when motive power departments were called upon to do the near impossible, that the Frisco's enginehouse forces still found time to scrub the road grime from every engine before it left on another run.

It was fitting and proper that the road exercise such care on its property, for the true student of steam motive power will agree that the Frisco was blessed with the handsomest variety of steam locomotives ever to roll across this continent. From its dainty little 4-4-0 American Standards to the big robust, company built 4-8-2's and dual service Northerns, three of them painted an eye catching blue for service on the *Meteor*, Frisco power was handsome and balanced.

The years just prior to 1950, however, saw rapid dieselization of the Frisco's main-line traffic. By the turn of the decade the famous Scullin disc drivered 4-8-2's and Baldwin built 4-8-4's with the "Frisco Faster Freight" phrase emblazoned on their tender sides sat mute and abandoned in the yards at Springfield and Memphis. It is ironic that while this modern power gathered rust, scores of smaller and older engines, some with World War I birth dates, still rolled splendidly over the single tracked iron with local freights and not a few passenger runs, especially on the lines radiating out of Memphis to St. Louis and Kansas City.

As the day of complete dieselization approached for many a road more and more attention was heaped upon the internal combustion units while the once faithful steam power arrived at home terminals with mud on their tender flanks and the grime of many days work encrusted on their drivers and were ignored in their hour of passing. Not so with the Frisco, even unto their last minute of operation the little Pacifics and Mikados were resplendent in new paint jobs, polished chrome bells and the like.

It was an exhilarating experience indeed to witness the southbound *Sunnyland* at sunup a few miles out of St. Louis on the southbound haul rolling majestically as of old across the Missouri foothills behind a sedate and prim little 4-6-2, its boiler agleam in the early sun while chrome plated rods flashed in arcs of reflected sunlight. It was enough to make one feel that this was forever, but as with all good things this too came to an end, and the spit and polish that was the byword of Frisco enginehouses is today but a legend.

With its brilliantly polished boiler jacket, chrome plated cylinder heads, and red painted number plate, and with its stack exhaust turning into a plume of white in the frost laden, early morning air, the Frisco's Mountain type No. 1500 charges out of the St. Louis yards like a knight in shining armor with the seven cars of No. 807, the *Sunnyland* on the first lap of its Memphis run.

After languishing in the St. Louis yards for fully an hour awaiting the passage of the morning southbound passenger haul, the *Sunnyland,* before pulling out on the main iron the Frisco's stout little 2-8-0 No. 1309 is following close on the markers of the fast disappearing varnish as it hustles south near Affton, Mo., with the River division's peddler freight No. 843.

One hundred cars of "redhots", California potatoes moving east in a hurry, are being whipped into motion east of Waynoka, Okla., behind the tall stacked drivers of Santa Fe 4-8-4 No. 3761. The fast moving spuds have already seen a variety of motive power at their helm. Growling V-16 diesels over the Sierras of California and across Arizona, ten coupled Santa Fe and Texas types over the hot New Mexico desert while now a fast stepping Northern has them in tow for a relay into the Argentine yards at Kansas City from there to finish their 2000 mile trek once again behind the guttural grumble of diesel power into Chicago.

Redhots

Familiar to most rail photographers who learned to keep tab on the seasonal upturns in the amount of active steam on many western railroads were the harvests of wheat, beets, and California perishables that brought about such revivals of steam power. None were as dramatic as the potato rush on the rails of the Santa Fe. Potatoes grown in southern California are sent east across the deserts with all possible urgency, racing to market the Idaho potato carried by the Union Pacific.

From the valleys around San Bernardino the long rows of orange and black S.F.R.D. refrigerators head east in 100-car trains rolling on schedules second only to first class varnish hauls.

In the summer of 1953 the harvest was good, but time was short and the solid blocks of potato laden reefers were being dispatched as fast as they could be mustered. Over the mountain ranges between California and Albuquerque four units of diesel power kept the wheels hot, but from the yards at Belen out and across the New Mexico desert to Clovis on the Santa Fe's Southern district, and thence to Amarillo and Kansas City, the potatoes rolled behind those steam driven giants of motive power, the Santa Fe's monstrous and fast, high drivered 2-10-4's and 4-8-4's.

With the urgency of wartime consists, on headways of less than ten minutes, the dripping refrigerators were double-headed upgrade through Abo Canyon and on east behind the 5000 class 2-10-4's as far as Clovis. From Clovis east to Amarillo and Kansas City the 80-inch drivers of the big 4-8-4's hit the 70 mark, and engineers accustomed to following close in the smoke of a previous lead section across the flat Texas panhandle roared through block signals only just changed from caution to clear without slackening their eastward pace.

It was a grand and glorious show of some of the finest steam power ever built and altogether fitting; in December 1953 the Santa Fe announced total dieselization. Though the steam thoroughbreds had not lost the potato race, they *had* lost the race with internal-combustion power.

Several of the 2-10-4's have seen occasional service since 1953 during the potato rush as helpers through Abo Canyon, but the big show is over. The orange reefers still roll east, though now behind the growling exhausts of V-16 power from California to Chicago. The haste is still evident, the schedules are as strict, but something is missing, and to those who loved steam that something was the show.

Above: Its rolling oil smoke exhausts blanketing the New Mexican desert, a tandem of Santa Fe superpower, 2-10-2 No. 3927 and 2-10-4 No. 5030, is thundering across the Rio Grande Valley south of Belen as it makes a run for the heavy grade through Abo Canyon. The train of 77 dripping refrigerators following in their wake is the first of four solid blocks of California potato specials running east on July 11, 1953.

The Abo Canyon grade is the Santa Fe's ruling eastward grade on the Southern district between Belen and Way-noka, Okla. In the days of steam it required the use of helpers on all tonnage trains.

At right: Its twin canopy of exhausts shadowing the surrounding terrain, the doubleheader of Santa Fe superpower is working all out on the last mile of grade through Abo Canyon. When the summit is reached at Mountainair, the 2-10-2 helper engine will be cut off, wyed, and returned light to the yards at Belen.

The 2-10-4 No. 5012 is assisted upgrade into Mountainair by four units of diesel power. Exactly a year later the situation was reversed. The 2-10-4's were assisting the diesel power upgrade! For although the Santa Fe achieved total dieselization in late 1953, the seasonal traffic build up in the summer of 1954 and 1955 saw several of the Texas types in service as helper engines over the Abo Canyon grade assisting diesel road power.

During the days of steam when potato specials such as pictured here and green fruit blocks were moving in numbers, the 40 miles of single track between Belen and Mountainair was a dispatcher's nightmare with lone helpers drifting downgrade and dodging in and out of passing sidings to avoid the long drags toiling to the summit.

Above, left: After cooling its flanges in the passing track at Ottawa Junction, Kansas, while several sections of a Boy Scout special ran around it, A. T. & S. F. No. 3752, a rebuilt Northern with Franklin rotary cam poppet valves, raises thunder as it exits from its temporary restraint with 102 "MT" orange reefers on their way west for loading.

Below, left: Stack extension in the uppermost position and flying green flags for a following section one of the Santa Fe's tremendous 4-8-4's, No. 3770, thunders west across the Kansas prairie near Olathe with a 99 car redball.

A second compressor is located just under the fireman's side of the cab, a quite unconventional location.

Above: The Santa Fe's impressively huge 2-10-4 Texas type No. 5014 surges across the New Mexico desert with a 72 car solid train of A. T. & S. F. refrigerator cars.

The Santa Fe broke the precedent of the 2-10-4 being a low drivered, drag freight engine when it ordered these engines built with 74 inch driving wheels, making them the highest drivered Texas types ever built.

While every transcontinental railroad hauled its freight over the western mountains with four cylinder articulated power, the Santa Fe steadfastly held to two cylinder engines.

Below: Near Black, Texas, Santa Fe's No. 2910 is shown roaring out of the east with stack up. A car on the parallel highway clocked this train at 75 miles an hour.

At left: Not only the largest of 4-8-4's but undoubtedly one of the finest steam locomotives ever built is justifiable praise for the Santa Fe's breed of Northerns. Specifically does this praise apply to the 3776-3785 class and the nearly identical group of 30 engines in the 2900 series built by Baldwin in 1941 and 1943. With 80 inch diameter drive wheels, an eight wheeled truck tender nearly equal to the engine itself in size, and a boiler a foot greater in diameter than that of any other 4-8-4, these engines look huge. Their full capabilities have never been unleashed. Sustained high speed runs of over 60 an hour with tonnage heavy trains were taken in stride. Notable among their achievements was the scheduled single engine run from La Junta, Colo., to Kansas City of the 18 to 20 heavy weight cars of the *Chief,* a distance of 540 miles where speeds frequently hit the 90 and 100 mark.

No. 3782 is here romping across the Texas Panhandle some 20 miles east of Clovis, N. Mex., at 65 mlies an hour with 92 loaded refrigerators..

Below: Its 84 inch drivers loping along, the Santa Fe's No. 3461 blankets the Kaw River bottoms near Bonner Springs, Kan., in a thick cloud of oil smoke as it thunders down the single track passenger main between Topeka and Kansas City with No. 28, the *Antelope.* This is one of the last runs to which the 3461-3465 series 4-6-4's were assigned.

No. 3463 of this group was donated to and put on permanent exhibit at the Kansas State Fair Grounds at Topeka. Though fitting monument it is, there is a certain something lacking in a steam engine sitting silent and motionless. For it is the sounds and smell of steam and hot grease that makes this machine a living, breathing thing with a personality of its own.

STEAM'S LAST ON THE "CHESSIE"

Left: Many are the safaris made by the author into the New River country of West Virginia in quest of the Chesapeake & Ohio's mighty H-8 class 2-6-6-6 type Allegheny articulateds, only, in all but a few instances, to find them standing mute and abandoned on a little used siding in either the Hinton or Clifton Forge yards. It was with the greatest of delight, therefore, that the news was received in early 1956 that due to an abnormal increase in the exporting of West Virginia bituminous coal to foreign ports, a number of these engines had been returned to service. Photographic equipment was mustered and another safari begun. The results of this attempt are here pictured.

A damp mist hung low in the New River Gorge which did little to dampen the spirits though as 2-6-6-6 No. 1624, its headlight casing askew, whistled off and came charging out of the Hinton yards with 161 empty hoppers rumbling behind.

The inclement weather was a fitting note though for news received the same day. Delivery of new diesel power had increased to such an extent that when the mines closed down for their annual vacation in June the fires would be killed in the mighty Alleghenies forever, and indeed they were.

Above: Hard put for motive power to move a record coal movement in the summer of 1955, the Chesapeake and Ohio not only took from the storage lines and put into service artciulateds and Berkshires but went so far as to steam up two of its beautifully proportioned Greenbrier 4-8-4's, the 610 and 614. Both of these engines went to work hauling coal drags between the pickup yards at Handley, W. Va., and the C. & O.'s huge classification center at Russell, Ky. This was a far cry from wheeling the *George Washington* or *Sportsman*, the job for which they were constructed in 1949. Though their length of service in coal hauling was brief, they were a welcome addition to the steam picture of that year as witness here the 610 rolling into Catlettsburg, Ky., with 86 empties for the West Virginia coal fields.

Noticeable is the lack of smoke exhaust, done deliberately in deference to the anti smoke ordinances regulated so strictly against railroads is the East which indirectly helped speed dieselization of several roads.

Out of the maze of track, switches, and multitude of cars that make up the Chesapeake and Ohio's giant classification yards at Russell, Ky., comes 2-8-4 type No. 2707 working east with 107 open top cars for the mines of West Virginia. No. 2707 is one of the highly successful designs of 2-8-4's built by American and Lima Locomotive Works for the C. & O. in the period 1943 to 1947.

Totaling some 90 engines in number, the 2700 K class sparked the movement of the engine headlight from the smokebox door to the pilot beam, which was continued on the road's newer Hudsons and Greenbrier 4-8-4's.

Disdaining the type name Berkshire for these engines, the Chesapeake & Ohio instead referred to them as the Kanawha type for the river whose banks the C. & O. main line parallels.

The Kanawhas or "Big Mikes" as the crews preferred to call them were notable in one other respect. Of all the successful, modern Lima designed 2-8-4's with 69 inch driving wheels, including those of the Nickel Plate Road, Louisville & Nashville, Wheeling & Lake Erie, and the identically designed five engines of the Virginian, the Kanawhas were given the highest tractive force rating, achieved through greater weight on drivers.

Shattering the solitude of an early Sunday morning at
Pratt, W. Va., a true Mallet compound No. 1506 of the
Chesapeake and Ohio pounds up the double tracked iron
headed for Cabin Creek Junction with 70 empty hoppers.
At Cabin Creek the thundering 2-6-6-2 will veer from the
main line and head up the branch to the mines at Red War-
rior, Cherokee, and Hazy Creek where its consist will be
spotted at the tipples for Monday loadings.

Its exhaust standing straight up in the calm of early morning air, Selkirk No. 5931 is near Medicine Hat, Alberta, with an eastbound extra.

"SELKIRK SECLUSION"

In addition to being the largest steam locomotive in the Canadian empire the Canadian Pacific's class T-1b 2-10-4 type Selkirks, a wheel arrangement generally employed only in heavy freight service, were the only 2-10-4's in streamline dress built expressly for dual service. Constructed by the Montreal Locomotive Works in 1938 and 1948 for service on the grades of the Canadian Rockies they were rarely seen east of Calgary, spending most of their life battling the grades of Kicking Horse Pass at the head end of such notable runs as the "Dominion" and the "Mountaineer".

An influx of dieselization in 1952 ousted them from their mountain domain causing them to be relegated to the task of hauling freight across the prairie provinces between Calgary, Medicine Hat, and Swift Current. During these recent years of reprieve on the prairies their ranks were constantly thinned since any heavy or expensive repair meant an automatic dismissal to the scrap line. When these photographs were taken in September 1956 there remained a mere six operating units out of the original sixteen engines.

Here is one of the lucky six, No. 5931, its streamlined sheet steel pilot replaced by a more conventional boiler tube affair, making a run for the eastward grade at Sidewood, Saskatchewan with 75 cars of time freight No. 980.

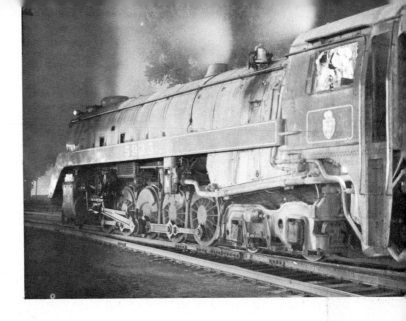

At right: The regal Beaver crowned crest of the Canadian Pacific in bright new paint on its cab side, the 5935 waits patiently in the night at Medicine Hat, Alberta, for the multi domed *Canadian* to arrive and depart. After the diesel drawn streamliner has cleared the westbound block, the 2-10-4 will follow it out toward Calgary with a 96 car stock extra.

At left: Rare in United States railroad operations, the 4-4-4 wheel arrangement was employed by the Canadian Pacific in passenger service throughout its system.

Here in the streamline dress peculiar to this Canadian road, a 4-4-4 No. 2916 sprints across the level prairie north of Weyburn, Saskatchewan, with a conglomeration of camp cars, freight, and combination mail and passenger cars that qualifies as mixed train No. 671 on the Moose Jaw-Cardrass run.

Below: Charging down a sag through Ernfold, Saskatchewan, the Canadian Pacific's oil burning No. 5387, a 2-8-2 more U.S.R.A. than Canadian in appearance, is hitting a breakneck pace across the rolling wheatlands.

Trailing the ever present auxiliary water tender behind its own tank, an Illinois Central 4-8-2 No. 2526 pounds across the Missisippi River bottoms a few miles out of East St. Louis, Ill., with 78 cars on the single track Springfield district.

Illinois Central Steam

SQUARE DOMES AND BARE BOILERS

Of all the main-line steam motive power to roll smokily and grandly across the American continent, that of the Illinois Central was probably considered the least photogenic. The road's adoption of large, square, box shaped sand domes in lieu of the more orthodox and accepted round shape astride the boiler, plus the mounting of air pumps on the pilot beam minus the customary and aesthetically valued shield which in itself lent identity to many a group of engines, were no doubt the greatest contributors to a design ranking far down on the list of photographic favorites.

Square corners and bare midriffs to the contrary, the old law of supply and demand did bring to Illinois Central steam power in the mid 1950's a period of rapt attention and publicity from railfans and publications alike, albeit all too short. It wasn't until the listings of roads completely dieselized had so increased that railfans desperate for the sight of valve motion and the smell of coal smoke began to turn to fields once overlooked. While other enginehouses heard only the ignominious honk of the diesel the lead tracks of I.C. roundhouses were bathed in soft coal smoke from scores of 4-8-2's, 2-10-2's, 2-8-2's, and such uncommon breeds as 2-10-0's and 0-8-2's. For the first time the square domes and exposed compressors became objects of interest and even affection.

The limelight was all too temporary, though, for even the Main Line of Mid-America had fallen to the ways of the diesel. A steady program of purchasing 50 to 75 new diesel units yearly began to show. By 1956 steam had been displaced on all the main lines of the Illinois Central, leaving only the branch lines to collect the soot from a passing 2-8-2.

By way of contrast, the branch line extending from the main line at Du Quoin to the coal mining community of Benton, Ill., which in years past rarely if ever fell under a camera lens, suddenly became the center of attention for desperate railfans from as far distant as New Jersey and Kansas. The two-stall enginehouse at Benton was host to two or three auto loads of railfans every weekend, arriving to record its sooty grandeur. Like all other reprieves for steam, though, this too was only temporary. Even as this is being written, the latest report is that this hidden haven for steam has succumbed to the diesel.

Whatever one's opinion may have been regarding the aesthetic values of Illinois Central steam power, the locomotives all had one argument in their favor. They were as steamy and as brawny a class of engines as ever existed and to watch one of the big Box Pok drivered 4-8-2's rolling across the Illinois prairies under a plume of soft coal smoke with the late evening sunset silhouetting its great barrel of a boiler is enough to cause one to dismiss aesthetic values for the moment.

At left: Although railroad tunnels in Illinois are quite rare, the Illinois Central's Edgewood Cutoff freight line through the southern part of the state has its share. To keep the maximum grade to .3% when the line was constructed in 1928 three bores were made through the Ozark foothills, all within a few miles proximity.

Of its three tunnels the most spectacular is the middle, designated appropriately enough tunnel No. 2. Over a mile in length, 6,985 feet to be exact, the tunnel is entered from either end through a solid rock walled approach cut some 85 to 90 feet deep and extending for a half mile from each portal. Accessible by motor vehicle only over rough back country dirt roads more fit for travel by sure footed donkeys, it is small wonder these bores are seldom visited by railfans.

Here is Illinois Central 2-10-2 No. 2743 which is drifting out of the north portal with 103 cars of First No. 70 North.

Below: While 4-8-2 No. 2525 cools its heels in the passing track at Stallings, Ill., with northbound freight No. 68, a sister Mountain type No. 2527 holds the main iron as it thunders by with 75 cars of St. Louis bound dispatch freight No. 67.

The Illinois Central built 56 of these big 4-8-2 types in its Paducah, Ky., shops between 1937 and 1942 using the boilers of ex 2900 class 2-10-2's mounted on a new one piece cast steel frame. Equipped with 70 inch Box Pok drivers, the engines soon proved to have the guts and gait to wheel both tonnage coal drags and redball merchandisers in stride across the level, prairie miles of Illinois.

Above: Mountain type No. 2417 is bringing the 15 cars of No. 16, the northbound *Seminole*, up a slight grade into the East St. Louis, Ill., station yards. Here the 4-8-2 will uncouple from the train and a Terminal Railroad of St. Louis switch engine will couple on and haul the consist backwards over the Mississippi River bridge to the St. Louis Union Terminal.

Below: Rolling with all the urgency of a redball time freight, the Illinois Central's smoke belching 2-8-2 No. 1257 is headed south at Kumler, Ill., with a single hopper and 47 empty grain cars on the single track St. Louis-Chicago main line.

Above: Although commonly referred to as Santa Fe types, after the road that originated the wheel arrangement the Illinois Central prefers to refer to its 2-10-2 engines as Central types.

Central type No. 2704 is here picking its way out of the East St. Louis, Ill., classification yards with a 98 car train of empty company hoppers.

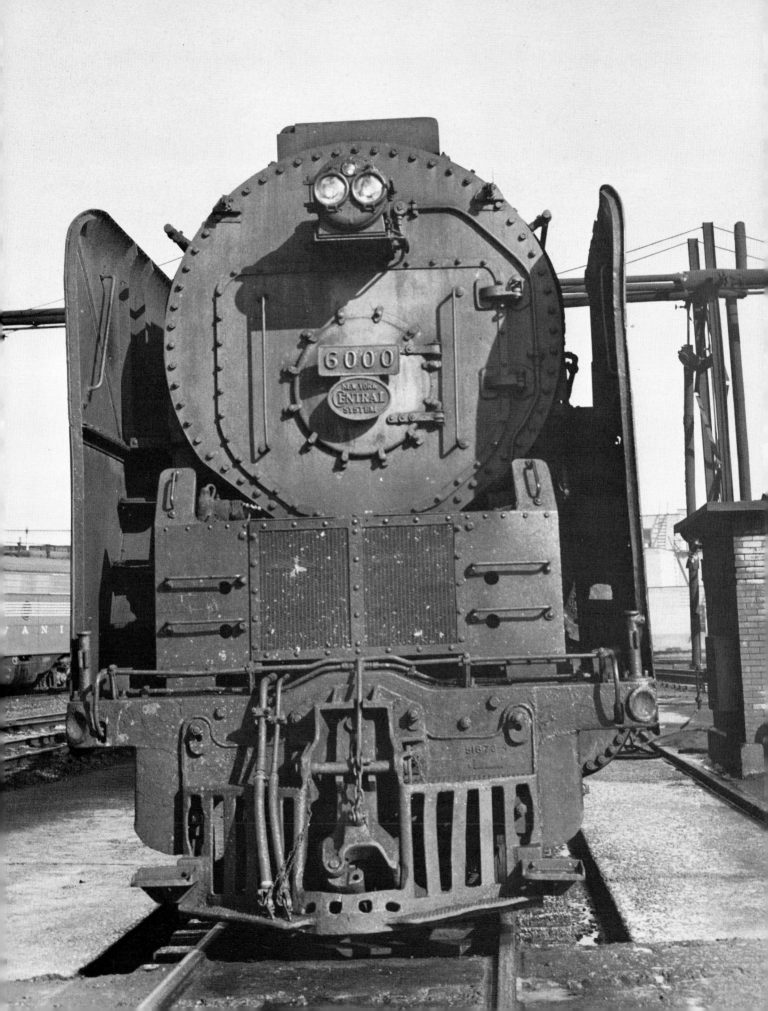

The Mighty Niagara

The most notable if not unique, modern dual service 4-8-4's to roll into the pre-diesel period of the 1950's were the New York Central's proud and publicized Niagaras. They were the Empire Route's only, though not the first, 4-8-4's and sported an exterior appearance that, while akin to New York Central thinking, was entirely unexpected.

Scorning the traditions set down by the aesthetically valued Mohawks and Hudsons, the 25 engines arrived from the builders, American Locomotive Works, in 1945 and 1946 with headlight held high on the smokebox front and a pair of stubby elephant ear smoke deflectors set close to a robust though beautifully turned boiler whose sand dome barely peered above its crest, while the steam dome was totally nonexistent. She was the biggest engine on the Central's rails; indeed, the biggest Central clearances could take.

The S-1a's, as they were classed along with the original S-1 class, No. 6000, and a class S-2a, No. 5500, which incorporated poppet valves instead of the more conventional piston type, soon set to work to break every established record for mileage and availability for any steam locomotive in the world.

In the 11-month period from May 1946 to March 1947 the 6024 of this great series amassed the amazing total of 228,850 locomotive miles in service. The Niagara was a leader in the dual type field. She was "the" steam locomotive of the world.

And yet inside of a mere decade she was just another relic of the dying age of steam. The inevitable had occurred. Electric traction motors replaced the hooked-up Baker motion of the S-1a's. Bumped by the insistent products of La Grange down through the ranks from one passenger haul to another, the Niagaras in 1954 and 1955 were to be found on rails and assignments far from the four track highway along the Hudson.

The majority wound up in Cleveland-Cincinnati service while a few even rolled into the Illinois division point of Mattoon at the head end of drag freights, ironically proving they were a dual service machine after all. Mattoon was as far west as they were allowed, their overall length of 115 feet being a little too much for the East St. Louis turning facilities.

After a ridiculously short life span the Niagara, too, joined the host of vanquished, the majority of the class being retired without ceremony in the steel mills at Granite City, Illinois.

At left: On one of the last first class assignments the Niagaras held, S-1a No. 6009 burns up the right of way at 80 miles an hour through Mauds, Ohio, in June 1954 with the 10 car, lightweight, gray-painted *Cincinnati Mercury* on the afternoon northbound run. Note how the engine's huge 42 ton capacity centipede tank dwarfs the lead car of the train.

Above: Its dual sealed beam headlamp imparting a somewhat "Martian" look to its countenance, S-1a No. 6025 leans to the curve at Berea, Ohio, with the 18 cars of No. 59, the westbound *Chicagoan,* in 1952.

The Niagara number series was derived from its 6000 horsepower rating.

Recorded here in a single photograph is the entire roster of equipment of the seven mile long Ferdinand Railway of Southern Indiana. A delicate limbed pre 1900 vintage American standard 4-4-0 No. 3 basks in the sun at Ferdinand, Ind., alongside the road's single piece of rolling stock, a one time Indiana Railway interurban car that sees duty as coach, caboose, and R.P.O.

No. 3 has been fired up and set outside while the crew telephoned the Southern Railway agent at Huntingburg to see if the larger carrier had perhaps set out a car on the interchange track for them to retrieve. A negative report was received whereupon the antique charge was dutifully returned to its one stall enginehouse to cool off and hope for better luck the next day.

When the Ferdinand's neighboring short line, the Corydon, turned to diesel power in 1953 the Ferdinand sold No. 3 to a Louisville scrap dealer and with the profits purchased the Corydon's No. 9, another 4-4-0 type with which, at last report, it still goes its merry and infrequent way.

Too Broke to Buy

The last steam locomotive in the United States will probably be retired not as a result of dieselization but because of the lack of funds to continue its operation. For this lone engine will undoubtedly be one of the score or more of antiquated Model T's of steamdom that still ply their weary way over the backwoods short lines of Arkansas, Louisiana, Georgia, and Tennessee. It is ironic that today after the most modern of dual service 4-8-4's, duplex drives, and articulateds have vanished by the hundreds, these leaking, long since worn out 2-6-2's, 4-4-0's, and Ten-wheelers, some of pre-20th century vintage, still make their daily except Sunday round trip between the backwoods communities that serve as home terminals and connections with the main line of the Mo Pac, Cotton Belt, or Southern.

Buried too deep both in the piney woods and debt alike to know the effects of dieselization, these remnants of a short-line empire all have one fact in common, a lack of finances sufficient to replace any but the most needed equipment. So they go their weary way in steam, the stacks of their ancient Ten-wheelers pouring forth clouds of honest to goodness smoke over a weed grown right of way whose rails dip precariously at their passage.

Some of the more financially stable roads have achieved total dieselization through, in most cases, purchase of a single small unit, a change for which these lines may well owe their continued existence. Exception rather than the rule applies here, and if past performance is any criterion, these remnants of a greater past will continue in steam until the day of complete abandonment, as evidenced in the recent throwing in of the towel by such familiar and loved shorties as the Sylvania Central, Smoky Mountain, and that little giant of short lines, the East Broad Top.

The operating routine of a short-line day is a timeless ritual, observed in like form by every member of the clan. The first sign of activity at any of these inconspicuous engine terminals is the arrival of the fireman at the first light of dawn to kindle a fire and begin the task of building up steam in the venerable steamer which has spent the night cold and oblivious to the snarl of GP-9's on a distant high iron. Steam up, the engine is fueled and inspected, those repairs needing no more than human effort effected, and then, leaking steam from every joint, the engine moves forth to assemble its train, or reasonable facsimile thereof, sans caboose, from what emptied or loaded cars that may be found on the usually not too numerous house tracks around town. Once the engine has a following the run is begun with a great show of courage, that is if courage can be measured in the amount of steam leaks, strident whistling, and the great shower of sparks put forth in departure.

The runs are usually slow and uneventful, length of the trip varying from a scant two miles as evidenced on the Augusta Railroad to the day consuming 20-mile run of the Arkansas Line. Frequent breakdowns and skirmishes with livestock grazing on the right of way are all taken in stride.

After a roller coaster trip over a proverbially undulating right of way, enlivened by not a few derailments, the aged Ten-wheeler, if it be such, emerges from the underbrush hiding the unballasted rail for a brief skirmish with the main-line connection, after which the lone engine makes off with its prize, be it a car of grain, lumber, or hardware.

Except for a chance stop at an adjacent farmhouse for fresh eggs, the down trip is as uneventful as the up trip, unless of course it be a Saturday in which case the crew, anxious to be home early for some week-end festivity, raps the stack of their ancient charge and goes bounding off over the rickety iron at a pace that must certainly end in self-destruction.

Having arrived safely once more at its sleepy home terminal, the lone car of revenue freight dropped with all due haste, and with its fires dropped and boiler growing cold, the ancient, once proud veteran of a mightier iron is bedded down for the night.

Blessed with what certainly must be the poorest highway system in the 50 states and a multitude of off the beaten path communities, it is small wonder that the state of Arkansas should abound with these little roads of yesteryear. Such heart warming pikes as the Augusta, the Reader Railroad, Prescott & Northwestern, and the archaic Arkansas Railroad itself still haul their daily except Sunday consists with steam as God intended. How long before the venerable steamers of these little lines meet the fate of younger cousins long since departed is a matter for conjecture and, for those who would enjoy a look back, haste is suggested.

At left: With 22 cars of coal from the mines at Robertsdale, the East Broad Top's little 80 ton Mikado No. 16 is making the last trip of the day over the road's three foot gauge rails to the washer and car dumper at Mt. Union, Pa. After depositing its tonnage train in the receiving yards, the 45 year old miniature behemoth will return to the roundhouse at Rockhill Furnace for the night.

Night is continuous now for No. 16 and its four sister engines slumbering away in adjacent stalls in the stone enginehouse. The closing of the mines at Robertsdale due to exhaustion of the coal reserves has ended operations on the East Broad Top. Although rails and equipment are stored intact pending a decision of the owner it is doubtful if this, the last common carrier narrow-gauge line east of the Rockies, will avoid the fate of so many predecessor short lines.

Above: The Louisville, New Albany & Corydon's red and silver trimmed 4-4-0 No. 9 is puffing mightily as it hauls an empty flat, three loaded box cars, and its bright red caboose up a slight grade and over State Highway 135 a few miles north of Corydon, Ind., in July of 1951 on its journey to its connection with the Southern Railway at Corydon Junction.

It was at this same crossing a few months later that the little line's newly purchased 70 ton diesel was nearly demolished in a collision with a loaded cement truck, thereby delaying the line's intended dieselization by several weeks.

Leaking steam from every joint, the Augusta Railroad's diminutive sized 2-6-0 No. 300, lettered for the jointly owned Arkansas Railroad, bravely sets out with two lone box cars in the early morning hours of a frosty March day in 1951 on one of its rare trips from Augusta, Ark., to the connection with the Missouri Pacific's Memphis-Little Rock main line, a scant two miles distant.

Life for No. 300 (pictured above and at right) ended very unceremoniously when in 1958 the little Mogul's boiler was condemned by a government inspector on a surprise visit, thereby trapping two foreign line cars on the little road's trackage in Augusta. A local farmer's tractor performed in the 300's place towing the two hapless box cars to the Mo Pac's interchange track and freedom.

Unable to afford financially the repairs to reinstate No. 300 in service, it is doubtful if the modernity of the diesel will transgress on the ailing steamer's stubby empire.

Left: Main line through Arkansas!

A plausible excuse for the 300's failings may be evident from the service, or more correctly, the lack of same at the Augusta enginehouse, a structure whose lazily tilted smoke-jack typifies the general state of affairs.

A dapper little Consolidation No. 4 of the Galesburg and Great Eastern, a 10-mile long short line of west central Illinois, is having a rough time of it attempting to drag tender first, 42 empty hoppers back to the Little John Coal Company tipple some five miles distant. To students of steam the 4-spot's ancestry is unmistakable — an ex Rock Island engine.

The red and white trimmed little 2-8-0 had brought a similiar train of loaded hoppers over the same right of way a few hours previous in pre dawn light to the Burlington's interchange track at Wataga. Now, with a strong side wind and a slight upgrade to contend with, the return trip has become considerably more difficult.

The Tuskegee's 2-6-2 No. 101 is charging down its 10 mile stretch of line toward the home terminal at Tuskegee, Ala., as though the very devil were chasing it. And well it might, for just moments before, while awaiting the arrival of the Western of Alabama's eastbound passenger haul at Chehaw station, its over ambitious fireman generously sprinkled the depot grounds, tinder dry in the August heat, with red hot cinders, thereby kindling a brush fire of minor proportions. Tho conflagration was quelled only by the heroic, broom swinging efforts of the station agent and several platform loafers down to see the train come in.

Its hurried flight was not without certain benefits, though, for in the still afternoon heat the breeze of its passage was enjoyed immensely by the train conductor, who lounged advantageously in a rocking chair in the doorway of the box car caboose trailing the run's consist of two well filled watermelon cars.

Above: A short but steep grade through a grove of pines in Blevins, Ark., has the Prescott & Northwestern's meticulously maintained, oil-burning 2-8-2 No. 17 working mightily as it hauls the seven cars and ex-Baltimore & Ohio caboose of the road's daily except Sunday train from Highland to Prescott, Ark., where it will interchange with the St. Louis-Texas main line of the Missouri Pacific.

The Prescott & Northwestern is possessed of yet another jewel of an engine, this one a well polished and fancy striped 2-6-2 No. 7 that substitutes on the run when No. 17 is ailing.

At right: A true daily except Sunday mixed, complete to its wooden combine, the Smoky Mountain's one and only rolls leisurely and smokily across the Tennessee uplands near Boyds Creek on its way between Knoxville and Sevierville behind what is surely the world's smallest 4-6-2 No. 110.

A short while before, the little Pacific had plunged head-long into a miniature avalanche of loose red mud washed into a shallow cut by heavy rains of the night before and it was only due to the combined efforts of the entire train crew and a lone passenger that the engine was extricated.

Nearly silent except for the sound of steam hissing from a dozen leaking joints, the Arkansas Railroad's antique, soot begrimed 2-6-2 No. 411 has all the appearance of a snake in the grass as it eases through a field of high grass and weeds on one of its infrequent trips over what is certainly the most decrepit 17 miles of right of way for any railroad, long or short.

When the photographer arrived at Star City, Ark., home terminus of the Arkansas Railroad, he was informed that the mixed daily had already departed for the other end of the line at Gould for a connection with the Missouri Pacific's main line. He was dutifully told, however, that although the train had left some two hours previous, it was surely no more than two or three miles out of town. A prompt search revealed that this was indeed the case.

As shown above, the train was to be found moving at considerably less than a snail's pace with nine foreign line cars whose owners would have had grave misgivings over having permitted their equipment to enter into such a perilous journey. And well they might, for the undulating and incredibly crooked rails of this little road would seem to make a journey over it nigh impossible.

Panting mightily to gain the top of a short grade along its roller coaster right of way, the Sylvania Central's tall-stacked ten-wheeler No. 103 is on the up run with the daily except Sunday mixed across the undulant Georgia terrain between Sylvania and Rocky Ford. The latter community, a piney woods settlement largely populated by free wheeling pigs, is notable in the Sylvania Central's operations as its connecting point with the Central of Georgia Railroad whose southbound passenger haul No. 108 the *Sylvania* endeavors to meet for interchange of mail, express, and whatever the larger road may offer in revenue traffic.

Above: The No. 103 waits on the side track at Rocky Ford while C. of G. Pacific No. 415 gallops out of town with the three cars of Savannah bound varnish.

The little 4-6-0 sat obediently for some time after the larger train had disappeared into the haze of the August noon, her master and pilot both bent on other errands. The conductor was intent on procuring a few dozen fresh chicken eggs from a nearby farm while the hoghead did his best to win the attention and amours, of a Georgia "miss" in a bright red dress who had been giving him the eye on his last several trips. His attempts were brought to a halt by the arrival of the conductor who, with arms loaded to the limit with egg crates, decreed that they should depart immediately for Sylvania.

The hoghead vented his wrath by charging full tilt upon a herd of bovines grazing contentedly upon the right of way who scattered in all directions upon the approach of the fire belching monster and its master. The conductor undoubtedly ate scrambled eggs for dinner that night.

The Sylvania Central passed into oblivion a few years later when the Central of Georgia purchased the Savannah & Atlanta, another Georgia short line which provided direct service to Sylvania, thereby making the existence of the Sylvania Central superfluous, or so at least to the C. of G.

There are those of us who would dispute that fact, however, for few short lines have been so typical and so quaintly beautiful in a location that time and the modernities of the twentieth century seemed to have ignored.

Two refugees from modernity repose in the evening's shadows seemingly discussing the events of the day on the abbreviated enginehouse tracks at Wadley, Ga. The large circular number plate on the smokebox of each engine identifying them as products of the Baldwin Locomotive Works of some distant year and both near identical Ten-wheeler types No. 53 on the left is the sole locomotive of the Wadley Southern which having just finished its daily trip to Swainsboro and return languishes quietly beside No. 43 which has earlier performed the same ritual on the rails of the Louisville and Wadley to Louisville.

Both of these piney woods roads are associated with a third short line of somewhat greater proportions, the Wrightsville and Tennille, and all three make a practice of borrowing coaches and locomotives from one another thus accounting for the appearance of No. 43, a W.&T. engine actually as attested to by the large W.&T. herald on its tender walls, being on the Louisville and Wadley's rails.

The frame structure to the left of No. 53, in a near state of collapse appearance wise, is the little lines equivalent of the main line coal tower except in this case the handle of the No. 7 scoop protruding from its topside is wielded by a sweating fireboy of color to fill the engine's tender bunkers each morning.

108

Making up in smoke and noise for what it lacks in size, the Interstate's chunky, little Consolidation No. 6 is pictured here as it takes a train of 31 empty hoppers out of Appalachia, Va., and literally and figuratively "up" the branch to the mine at Osaka.

Located in the forest covered mountain reaches at the very tip of Virginia's westernmost boundary, the Interstate's rails are accessible for photography in only limited locations, and indeed it seems this very inaccessibility has made the management more than hospitable to railfans who wander in intentionally or otherwise.

The Appalachian ridges were not barrier enough, though, to keep out the brush beating internal combustion salesmen, for even at this early date in 1952 there was talk in the little enginehouse at Appalachia of impending dieselization.

In the picture above, No. 6 wraps both its stack exhaust and train of empties around a bend in the rails as it tackles the 2% out of Appalachia.

Above, left: Litchfield and Madison Railway meant 40 miles of single track between a fair sized yards at Madison, Ill., to rails end at Litchfield, where connection was made with the Burlington's Beardstown division. Some 26 miles north of the Madison yards a branch extended off to connect with the Chicago & Northwestern's Nelson district at Benld which produced the bulk of L. & M. tonnage. This segment provided a direct Chicago-St. Louis connection for the C. & N. W. and was the reason for the short line's merger with the larger system in 1958.

The No. 161 is steaming away on a quiet Sunday afternoon at the Edwardsville enginehouse track.

Below, left: The Akron, Canton & Youngstown, a short line with main-line overtones that begins in a small yard at Delphos, Ohio, and crosses the whole of the state to Akron, was, at the time of this exposure, wholly dieselized with the exception of its daily except Sunday mixed local No. 45, which though principally a local freight, carries an honest to goodness wooden combine.

Here No. 45 rolls cautiously behind a 2-8-2 No. 406, whose beautiful design and meticulous maintenance would shame many a larger, main-line carrier.

Above: Its twin eyed sealed beam headlight peering into a rain dampened countryside, a fat-boilered 2-8-2 of the coal hauling Montour Railroad clatters across the strip mine area of Pennsylvania headed for Imperial.

The Montour's shops and enginehouse facilities are hidden in a narrow defile at Coroapolis, Pa., where it makes connection with the Pittsburgh & Lake Erie's main.

Above: The little 1-spot of the Mike 'n Ike is panting mightily on the grade between Desloge and Bonne Terre, its stack talk sounding not at all unlike "I can make it, I can make it." Its train includes all of 11 cars.

Mike 'n Ike

A subsidiary of the Missouri Pacific System and referred to locally as the Mike 'n Ike, the Missouri-Illinois acts as a bypass around the busy St. Louis terminal for freight moving between the east and southwest. The road was conceived to serve the giant St. Joseph lead mines in the vicinity of Flat River, Mo., and to this day gets much of its income from this traffic. While the majority of its trackage and most scenic operations are in the state of Missouri, its rails do extend as far east as Centralia and Salem in central Illinois. It is in this area that the road has a score or more of oil wells along its right of way from whence it derives considerable profit.

The winding of its rails amid the Ozark ridges of Missouri and the short trains behind little engines on steep grades was reminiscent of the days of the Colorado Midland. On the branch to Leadwood, Mo., over which only the lightest power dare venture, there was even a mountain climbing switchback. Until late in the 1930's, the little road even boasted passenger service behind a pair of miniature Pacifics.

As if this were not enough to endear it to the hearts of visiting railfans, the crossing of the mighty Father of Waters is accomplished in a manner as rare as today's steam locomotive itself. A side-wheeler car ferry, the *Ste. Genevieve*, plies back and forth just north of the town of Ste. Genevieve itself, ferrying 18 cars at a time across the muddy waters. Loading and unloading is accomplished on each side of the river by a 2-8-0 reaching out from a floating dock with a way car to avoid the engine's weight crossing onto the boat. Railroad car ferries have largely disappeared from the American scene, making this operation a rarity indeed.

With one exception the Missouri-Illinois has moved its tonnage during its life in steam with nothing larger than a 2-8-0. The antiquated, dirt floored backshops at Bonne Terre, Mo., were the recuperation center for a score of little spot numbered 2-8-0's from the miniature No. 7 pictured making the last run of its career in July 1951, to the heavier secondhand engines acquired from the Missouri Pacific in recent years. The lone exception referred to above was a miniature sized 2-8-2 used principally in mine service duty at Salem, Ill.

Disregarding the three miles of trackage rights over the Illinois Central at Centralia, Ill., the entire system is laid with relatively light 90 pound rail, this being sufficiently heavy for motive power of such diminutive size. The light rail was no deterrent to the use of diesel road switchers however and being of sound financial status the little road joined with its parent, the Mo-Pac in complete dieselization in mid 1950.

Above: During the twenty odd years before its abandonement in mid 1950 passenger service on the Mike n' Ike consisted of a gurgling and gruesome appearing gas electric railcoach and an R.P.O. trailer operated on the Illinois side of the Mississippi River between river's edge and the eastern extent of the line at Salem. When the fire-spitting contraption was ailing and laid up for repairs, an all too frequent occurence, a freight locomotive saw double duty as substitute power. While the line was yet in steam in 1952 Consolidation No. 154, on loan from the Mo Pac, wheels the substitute abbreviated consist up to the toylike water tank at Evansville, Ill. for a drink of ole' man river.

Above, right: No. 24 is busily engaged in unloading the Mississippi River car ferry near Ste. Genevieve. The semaphore signal guards a crossing with the Frisco Line's River division rails over which the 2-8-0 must cross each time to deposit its load in the receiving yards.

Today the car ferry still operates daily, only a blue and white Alco hood unit does the honors now. The grades and curves still abound but the happy sounds of steam railroading in the Missouri Ozarks are stilled forever on the Mike 'n Ike.

Below: The 1898 vintage Consolidation No. 7 makes a frantic run for the grade near Desloge, Mo., with nine cars tied to its minute tank.

The Displaced EM-1's

Dieselization and its inherent retirement of competing steam power inevitably meant the scrapman's torch for any engine custom built for the job on which internal-combustion units were replacing it. In several instances, however, certain classes of steam power, by virtue of their modernity or length of boiler time remaining, were spared the death sentence and given a reprieve through reassignment to some division or branch line other than their original tailored position. Thus it was that steamers which were custom built and assigned to one operation since their birth put in their appearance on a distant as yet nondieselized district.

Although always of a temporary nature, each stay of execution was fortunate in that it afforded the photographers of steam a chance not only to record these engines in a new domain but more time in which to relish their existence.

Instances of note were the sudden and brief appearance on the New York Central's lines west of Bellefontaine, Ohio, of the seven Alco built Pittsburgh & Lake Erie 2-8-4's, which heretofore had never strayed from the rails of their parent road, or the assignment of the Baltimore and Ohio's proud President class Pacifics to hauling mail and express locals over the St. Louis division after a lifetime at the head end of such notables as the Capitol Limited, Royal Blue, and Cincinnatian; and of course the change that attracted the most notice, the leasing of 17 Santa Fe line 2-10-4's by the Pennsylvania in 1956 for hauling coal on the Sandusky-Columbus Line.

Such was the fortunate case with the Baltimore & Ohio's 2-8-8-4 class EM-1 articulateds. The 30 engines of this group were built by Baldwin in 1942 specifically to handle the heavy wartime swollen tonnage that had to be hoisted over the Allegheny Mountains west of Cumberland, Md., by way of the famous 17-Mile and Cranberry grades. Up to V-J Day and on into the early 1950's this handsome breed of articulated steam power ruled supreme on this mountain district, handling coal drags and main-line hotshots alike.

By 1953, however, the growl of internal-combustion units had become too ominous to be ignored. Occurring at a time when many of the road's familiar S-1a class 2-10-2's were badly in need of heavy repairs due to years of constant and heavy use throughout the eastern end of the system, it became advantageous to replace the ailing Santa Fe types on the heavier trafficked coal branches with the newer and more powerful articulateds. Thus a goodly portion of the EM-1's went to work on a coal originating branch in eastern Ohio that heretofore had evoked little if any railfan interest.

With a spacious frame enginehouse that would seem more appropriate for a main-line division point and a lengthy yards tucked neatly away among the hills at Holloway, Ohio, this line originates coal from the numerous strip mines nearby and feeds it north to the lake port at Lorain in 8000-ton trains.

The popularity that the EM-1's brought to the little known engine terminal was attested to by the emptied film cartons scattered profusely among the cinders of the enginehouse lead tracks. The popularity of the EM-1 among railfans is justly due, for in a wheel arrangement not usually recognized for its handsomeness of design the EM-1 has no peer; its cleanness of lines, well proportioned boiler and cab, and all welded tank make it the beau brummel of articulateds.

The big Yellowstones were well at home in this service and seldom did one sit idle when coal traffic ran heavy. Although there are no grades near comparison with those the EM-1's were accustomed to further east in the Alleghenies, there are several ascending grades between Holloway and Warwick of sufficient proportions to cause a single EM-1 with an 8000-ton train to knuckle down and fight with every ounce of steam, a sight reminiscent of smoke filled skies west of Cumberland. Between Strasburg and Justus where the B.&O. line intersects the double track iron of the Nickel Plate Road is the stiffest grade, and if perchance the crossing is occupied by a Nickel Plate drag bringing a northbound tonnage train to a halt, the slamming of drawbars and slipping of drivers is ear pounding indeed as all 16 drivers do their utmost to urge 8000 tons of dead weight into motion.

At Warwick, Ohio, the branch merges and loses its identity with the Akron district of the Chicago division and the EM-1's then rolled west on the double track iron as far as Sterling, a distance of 20 miles. Here they swung off the main iron and onto the Lorain subdivision to head north again for that lake port, which this author feels merits the dubious distinction of being the dirtiest engine terminal he has yet come across.

At summer's end in 1957 the EM-1's still exhausted uninterruptedly from the yards at Holloway. Constant use and little attention other than end of the run servicing had left the engines dirty and ill maintained—conditions that normally make for the entrance of diesel power. It was the business recession of 1958, however, that put the EM-1's to pasture and allowed their arch enemy the diesel to enter their final reservation.

In the glory of their reprieve, though, the EM-1's are here recorded.

TABLE MANNERS AT HOLLOWAY HOUSE

The ample roomed, board enginehouse at Holloway, though squeezed into a narrow defile in the eastern Ohio hills, has housed the largest of Baltimore & Ohio steam power. The early Mallets were its first tenants, and after the EM-1 articulateds came to Cumberland and 17 Mile Grade, the 2-10-2's released from helper service there took up a new lease at Holloway.

Finally, replaced in turn by throbbing V-16 diesels on the Appalachian grades, the EM-1's themselves came to join their predecessors in the Holloway boardinghouse. The stalls at Holloway will no doubt be the last residence of this fine breed of articulated power and the aged, fading red wooden stalls will join in passing from the American railroad scene with the machines they housed.

Here, silhouetted against a noon sky, one of the star boarders of Holloway house is 2-8-8-4 No. 7606, fighting for every inch on the ascending grade south out of the yards with 117 empty hoppers destined for the nearby strip mines.

119

The same train as seen on page 116 behind the 655 is pictured here in a more leisurely attitude rambling smokily across a fill near Midvale, Ohio in the early afternoon.

Though personal preferences may differ, the Baltimore & Ohio's EM-1 2-8-8-4's are generally considered as the handsomest of articulated designs. Justification of this praise is evident indeed in the pair of cross-compound air pumps housed behind rolled shields similar to those of a dual service 4-8-4, and the clean, symmetrically tapered boiler ending in the roomy cab merited by an engine of this size. All of this mounted on 63 inch diameter Box Pok drivers and trailing a smooth sided, all-welded tank very nearly makes the EM-1 peer to none.

Railfans, however, are a critical lot with tastes as varied as the weather so the title is not without challenge. The viewer is, however, asked to witness and ponder as in the photograph above EM-1 No. 672 rolls ponderously out of a sag near Grafton, Ohio, at close to 40 an hour on the southbound run with 123 "MT's".

At left: Leaving its train of 119 coal filled hoppers a mile south of town on the Holloway branch, EM-1 No. 7604 has run light over the Akron division main line to the coal chute at Warwick, Ohio, filled its tender, returned to its waiting train, and now under a tremendous cloud of soft coal smoke charges under the concrete coaling tower and west out of town at 30 an hour.

With the near-dirt quality of coal heaped into the Mallet's bunkers, it is small wonder that the engine should smoke so!

Above: After waiting somewhat impatiently next to the home signal at the Warwick, Ohio, interlocking while three eastbound *Sentinel* freights growled through behind a multitude of diesel units, the Baltimore & Ohio's S-1 class 2-10-2 No. 6120 strains forward in a sudden burst of energy to get across the interlocking and gain the safety of the westbound main. The train is a daily run mixture of coal and general merchandise up from Holloway, which will now run on the main iron as far west as the division point at Willard.

Truly the last in steam on the Burlington Route. O-5a No. 5632 endeared herself and the Burlington to the hearts of hundreds of steam locomotive admirers thru its retention in service for use on railfan specials and excursions trips long after all other "Q" steamers had fallen from the active list. Here are some 400 happy, shutter snapping railfans reliving a happy yesteryear as the grand old lady roars thru Oneida, Ill., at close to 80 an hour with 13 cars of a Chicago Railroad Club Special on April 5, 1959.

The photographer standing some distance down the right of way is indicative of the hundreds of such faithful followers who lined the route between Chicago and Galesburg to pay homage to this now revered patriarch of steam.

The Burlington

A GRANGER ROAD IN STEAM

The survival of steam on many a railroad can be credited to the seasonal surge of traffic that hits every road at one time of the year, whether it be the ore traffic of the Missabe Road while the Great Lakes are ice free in the summer months, the potato rush of the Santa Fe, or the heavy wheat and grain rush that makes everything with wheels begin to move on the midwestern roads in midsummer. The Chicago, Burlington & Quincy belongs to this latter crowd of midwestern granger roads. For though this suddenly increased tonnage is a blessing to the pocketbook, it is a curse to the motive power department which must keep a reserve of power ready to meet the demands of increased schedules. Since it is pure heresy to keep an expensive diesel idle during the winter months waiting for such traffic rushes, most of the railroads susceptible to this traffic held their best conditioned steam power in storage during the lean winter months while letting the newly arrived and expensive diesels handle normal winter traffic needs. The Burlington is notable in this respect because it held to this practice long after other of the wheat belt roads purchased enough diesel power to protect against such increases.

It is to the Burlington's credit that when the wheat combines began to move north into Nebraska and the beets in northeastern Colorado were ready for harvest, there emerged from the enginehouses at Galesburg, Ottumwa, Council Bluffs, and Lincoln, Nebr., some of the most lovingly tended steam motive power to be found during the age of dieselization. The great O-5a 4-8-4's of the Burlington's own making again made the night musical with the melancholy whistle peculiar to "Q" steam power.

The summer of 1955 was no exception to the rule on the Burlington's rails. A bountiful harvest was in full swing on the Nebraska prairies and in the absence of diesel power sent to further west divisions steam once again held sway in the enginehouses at Galesburg and Lincoln. Not only were O-5a's dispatched regularly on these lines but rarest of rarities, a live 4-6-4 Hudson could be found wheeling freight between Omaha and Lincoln as seen on the pages following.

Like all steam power reactivation this was a temporary thing. The day came when even the largest grain harvest couldn't coax forth a live 4-8-4. Even as the snows began to blow across the plains in late November and the last dispatched O-5a was put to sleep for the winter, it was doubtful if there would be an awakening in the spring. New diesel power brought even this temporary show to a halt.

Hard pressed for serviceable freight power during the bountiful grain harvest of 1955, the Burlington saw fit to put into action a lone 4-6-4 Hudson on the Lincoln-Omaha district. This fortunate choice was the 79 inch drivered No. 4002 which had been sitting silent in the Lincoln roundhouse for several months.

Its quiet sojourn in storage had not been without attention though as evidenced in the polished boiler lagging and roller bearing rods.

The 4002 was no stranger to freight service, having been used frequently on fast carded merchandise runs between Chicago and Galesburg for several years prior to its storage at Lincoln.

Here, some 20 miles out of Lincoln, Nebr., the oil burning 4-6-4 is scorching the ballast with a 74 car stock extra.

The 4-8-4 Northern type was always a popular and successful locomotive on the granger roads of the Middle West. She rambled across the prairies of Illinois and the undulating farmlands of Iowa, Kansas, and Nebraska with wheat trains, stock extras, and merchandise runs alike. She was no stranger to passenger hauls either and her eight big disc drivers could make time with 18 to 20 heavyweight Pullmans.

To the biggest of grangers, the Burlington Route, this wheel arrangement was no stranger. Besides eight 4-8-4's built by the Baldwin Locomotive Works in 1930, the "Q"

itself built 13 Northerns in its own West Burlington shops in 1937, the 5608-5620 class, and was so well pleased with their performance as to build 15 more in 1938-40. The appearance of this group, Nos. 5621-5635, differed from earlier classes mainly in the application of a solid, sheet steel pilot with retractable coupler, all-weather cab, though generously endowed with glass area, and a pilot shield covering the Worthington Feedwater heater pump on the pilot beam. The engines of this last group, the greatest of the "Q's" justifiably famous 0-5a Northerns, were among the last steam power to be used on the granger road.

At Oneida, Ill., on a crisp October day in 1955 the Burlington's great 0-5a 4-8-4 No. 5624 charges over the high speed iron toward the Galesburg classification yards at close to 60 an hour with 122 cars of Chicago originated merchandise.

A Burlington U.S.R.A. heavy Mikado of the 5500-5510 series, pressed into grain movement service in 1955, pounds over the single track iron near Greenwood, Nebr., with 86 empty grain cars headed for prairie town elevators.

The Die-Hards

At summer's beginnings in 1958 the diesel-electric invader had become a part of railroading in the United States to such an extent that the number of roads yet operating steam power of any consequence could be counted on the fingers of one's hand. These rebellious die-hards even then were operating on borrowed time, their dates of retirement already forecast for the near future. In fact one of these rebels, notably the Nickel Plate Road, after starting the year with a hopeful promise of continuing steam operations, had hardly entered into the season before the sounds of steam were silenced on its rails.

Those roads yet operating steam power at this time, five in number, represented a hodgepodge of variety in traffic, operating conditions, and types of motive power in service. East of the Mississippi there were three holdouts—as mentioned before the Nickel Plate Road, and as to be expected the road that once boasted of its continued confidence in steam, the coal hauling Norfolk and Western.

In the case of the Nickel Plate, the year unfolded with a bright promise of continued life for the famous Lima built S-4 class 2-8-4's, at least on the division between Ft. Wayne, Ind., and Chicago where the lack of Centralized Traffic Control nullified any advantageous use of automatic train control equipped diesel power. Over the undulating, single track right of way across northern Indiana the Nickel Plate's famous 96 and 98 fast freights hit their stride behind the staccato exhaust of the big and beautifully designed Berkshires. East of Ft. Wayne the striped face Alcos and GP-9's held sway, but west of the small busy yard, steam seemed entrenched for some time to come.

The time to come was not long in arriving. Down in the New River country of West Virginia, the Chesapeake & Ohio Railroad, its coal traffic in a decline in accordance with the general business decline of the country, suddenly found itself in the undesirable position of having excess diesel power in storage. The Nickel Plate's management, seeing an opportunity to dieselize the last steam operated segment of the system, took quick action. Leasing arrangements were made with the C. & O. and on June 14th the first 25 of 35 leased road switchers arrived at Ft. Wayne for use on the Chicago Division. As each unsuspecting 2-8-4 arrived hot and steaming with a trainload of merchandise just out of Chicago it was sent to the enginehouse, its fires dropped and the engine placed in dead storage in a manner that appears to be permanent.

By Sunday evening of the 15th the last Berkshire was put to rest and thus another steam stronghold fell. On the pages following in this section the memorable 2-8-4's are shown in their glory, both in action on various other divisions of the Nickel Plate and at Ft. Wayne only hours before retirement.

Holed up along the banks of the Tug Fork River in the hills of eastern Kentucky and West Virginia in a manner reminiscent of the Hatfield-McCoy feud which once brought this area notoriety, the steam rebels of the Norfolk and Western staged their last holdout. The famous utilitarian designs of the road, the Y-6b 2-8-8-2's and class A 2-6-6-4's worked the Pocahontas coal east and north to ocean and lake ports in 175 car trains as late as 1958.

While the somber black painted GP-9 hood units had gained complete control of all but two divisions of the N. & W. iron by late 1958 and handled most of the plush merchandise runs, plus even bumping the streamlined J class 4-8-4's off the Powhatan Arrow and Pocahontas, the A's and Y's still moved the West Virginia coal either east from Roanoke to tidewater or west from Williamson to the retarder yards at Portsmouth, Ohio. Even now operating on a limited basis with steam, these two steam strongholds are expected to fall momentarily and their existence may well be terminated at the time of this publication.

Nowhere in raildom has more surprise been evoked than over the rapidity with which the Norfolk & Western has carried out its dieselization program. Long after several EMD test units had been given a workout on the property in 1952, the management stoutly denied any desire to join the ranks of its coal hauling brethren such as the rapidly dieselizing Chesapeake & Ohio and stood by its unconditional loyalty to steam.

In 1956, however, the management itself let the camel push his nose into the tent with its decision to place eight hood units in service on the Lynchburg-Durham branch, ironically enough to allow use of the heavy steam power then in use to be employed elsewhere on the main iron. The units had hardly been broken in when the road announced its intent to acquire more of the same motive power for use on other branches. Within a few months the road had completely reversed its motive power policy, announcing that the diesel was there to stay and steam was on the way out.

Lacking in publicity but nevertheless harbouring quite a number of live steamers, the Grand Trunk Western moved into the summer of 1958 with not a few freight runs still headed with steam power and a considerable number of commuter runs out of Durand and Detroit, Mich., still sporting such orthodox power as 4-8-2's and 4-6-2's. The Grand Trunk's seeming reluctance to dieselize stems from the fact that its parent road, the Canadian National, has set a probable date of 1960 for complete system wide dieselization and the Grand Trunk seems included in this forecast.

The olive green and gold striped 4-8-4's no longer wheel the *Maple Leaf* grandly out of Chicago as depicted on the pages following but ignominiously follow a pair of EMD "hood" units east each morning. As this is written, the suburban runs in and around Detroit still command a steam engine, though, and put on quite a little show of their own.

North of the headwaters of the Mississippi, in the red earth country of northern Minnesota there can yet be heard an occasional muttering of steam from a road that once teemed with the heaviest of motive power. The Duluth, Missabe & Iron Range Railroad, its enginehouses once hot from the breath of such behemoths as 0-10-0's, 0-10-2's, 2-8-8-4's, and 2-10-4's, still shows an infrequent sign of life with the dispatching of one of its few operating Yellowstone types out of the yards at Two Harbors, Minn., with a string of empty ore hoppers for the open pit mines at Virginia and Hibbing. The occasions were not only infrequent but most likely to occur at night, a circumstance known to give heart failure to the serious minded rail photographer.

With steel production down considerably in 1958 from the all time highs of 1953 and 1955, the Missabe Road found itself with a surplus of motive power on

132

hand. Having just embarked on a dieselization program in 1956, the road was quick to set aside in storage all the steam power it could spare. Leasing of over a score of diesel units from the Great Northern which had found itself in the same unhappy situation of decreasing ore traffic, along with the importation of several more diesel engines from its United States Steel controlled brethren, the Bessemer & Lake Erie, brought about near dieselization of the entire road.

Rows of cold and silent outside motion motive power appeared in the yards at Proctor, reminiscent of the winter months when all ore traffic comes to a halt on the Missabe and motive power is stored until the lakes thaw in the spring. This time, though, the storage seems permanent.

The 2-8-8-4's that roll more and more infrequently from the yards at Two Harbors are on stand-by call only. The little 4-6-2's that once rolled the Missabe Road's little jewel of a passenger train complete with diner and solarium observation from Duluth into the iron range country have already felt the torch, and a like fate for their big brothers seems close at hand. The sounds of steam on the Missabe Road are scarce and promise to become more so in the not too distant future.

At the beginning of this text the die-hards in steam were listed as five and of these the majority were staging their last ditch fight east of the Mississippi. What then of the far-flung lines of the western United States and its motive power of towering proportions? In all the reaches of the wide, wide West there was but one slight trace of smoke on the horizon. It spewed forth in amounts all out of proportion to the size of the motive power in whose innards it was created.

The Denver & Rio Grande Western's diminutive outside frame 2-8-2's, toiling laboriously up from Alamosa and Durango into the heights of Cumbres Pass over the last remaining three-foot gauge right of way in the country, were ironically enough the sole survivors of steam in the western states in 1958. True enough, the beet harvest of northern Colorado might bring to life for a few weeks motive power of greater proportions on the Colorado & Southern or the Great Western, and even the mighty Union Pacific might be forced to fire up a steamer or two, but for any consistent amount of performance in steam in 1958 and 1959 the three-foot Rio Grande was it.

The most ironic fact of all was that with the exception of the Grand Trunk Western's commuter runs, the last remaining regularly scheduled passenger run in the U. S. was over the Rio Grande's narrow spaced rails into the mountain vastness at Silverton. A tourist attraction, to be sure, operated only in the summer months, the Silverton run substantially remains an honest to goodness varnish run in steam.

There is little reason to dwell at great length on the past and future of the Rio Grande three-foot gauge, for with all the fine publications in existence devoted to the wanderings of this line and others in the Colorado Rockies whatever the author would have to say would be merely a rehash. Suffice it to say that the slim gauge is still delightfully in steam and would appear to remain so since the management in Denver seems quite reluctant to invest any more than absolutely necessary to maintain operations over the line, therefore hopefully forestalling any purchase of diesel power. Should steam operations come to an end on this line it appears as though it will only be through complete abandonment of the entire narrow gauge system.

At left: S-4 Berkshire No. 768 is talking to the world as she accelerates across the level farmlands east of Ft. Wayne with 126 cars of drag freight. One of the truly beautiful engines of our time finishing out life the only way she knows how — in thunderous ovation!

At right: Synonymous with Norfolk & Western are the trains of clanking black coal hoppers emerging from the West Virginia mountains in a seemingly endless number. Completely out of harmony with this picture is this 103 car solid block of refrigerators being hurried east near Elliston, Va., fast as the stubby 57 inch drivers of 2-8-8-2 No. 2168 will roll.

135

At left: Carrying green markers for a following section, the Nickel Plate's westbound time freight No. 45 is an apt witness to the road's boast of high speed freight service as it streaks across the American bottoms near Peters, Ill., under the billowing exhaust of Berkshire No. 706.

Above: The water level in its tender a scant two feet from the empty mark as evidenced by the sweat line, the Nickel Plate's big 2-8-4 No. 730 is about to thunder across the Illinois Central's diamond at Glen Carbon, Ill., with 85 cars of second No. 49, East St. Louis bound time freight.

One of the most potent weapons with which the diesel scored on the Norfolk & Western was its ability to run by water stops that steam power dare not ignore. Having reduced stops for hotboxes to a record low, the operating department went all out to reduce the number of these water stops. Stopping and starting the 13,000 ton trains which the N. & W. is accustomed to run is costly and time consuming. All main-line freight power blossomed out with auxiliary water tenders early in 1953 constructed from older engine tanks, thus eliminating all intermediate terminal water stops. Although a very practical and efficient solution to the problem where steam power was concerned, the diesel designers' solution looked even better. When the first hood units ignored every water plug on the system, the management saw immediate solution to an age old problem.

In the photograph above a class A 2-6-6-4 No. 1207 sports a 16,000 gallon auxiliary water tank as supplement to its own tender's capacity as it rolls north near Waverly, Ohio, with a tonnage train of 160 loaded coal hoppers, a total tonnage of 13,000.

Above: Berkshire No. 814 of the Nickel Plate Road walks 95 empties up the heavy duty iron east out of the Brewster, Ohio, yards. The 814 is a former 6400 class 2-8-4 of the Wheeling & Lake Erie acquired by the Nickel Plate when the two roads merged. Renumbered in the 800 series to conform as a continuation of the Nickel Plate's own 700 class 2-8-4's, the 800's were a short lived group.

The 814 is unusual in that it was one of the few modern 69 inch drivered Berkshire designs to sport footboards instead of a conventional pilot, the footboards obviously being of more value to the head end crew than the small steps of a standard pilot when switching the numerous coal mines served by the road in western Pennsylvania and eastern Ohio.

At right: 0-10-2 No. 607 is attacking a grade with 65 empties. No. 607 is one of nine such engines purchased from the Union Railroad of Pittsburgh, Pa., when that road became dieselized. A special design for the Union Railroad, constructed for transfer and switching of heavy ore trains in the Pittsburgh steel mill area, the 607 is right at home at the same job on the Missabe Road.

This was not the first purchase of motive power from the Pittsburgh area for the Missabe. The 700 class of 2-10-4's, were received secondhand from the Bessemer & Lake Erie.

At left: From the sprawling riverside hump yard at Portsmouth to the end of Norfolk & Western trackage at Columbus, Ohio, lie 98 miles of heavy-duty double track iron. Officially the Scioto division (pronounced See-o-toe) and named for the water level river valley which it traverses, this 152 pound rail sees the heaviest of N. & W. coal traffic. Both tonnage trains of coal and empties moving south seldom average under 175 cars.

The class A 2-6-6-4 locomotives used exclusively on this division were ideally suited to this service. Equipped with 70 inch drivers for speed, a generous boiler capacity, and consequent high horsepower rating, they were capable of maintaining a steady 40 to 50 an hour gait nonstop from terminal to terminal with a 13,000 to 14,000 ton coal train.

Although apt to raise eyebrows on any other railroad, the length and tonnage of these Scioto division coal drags were quite matter of fact to the Norfolk & Western. The interminable passage of one of these two mile long drags past a viewer is apt to leave him either fascinated or annoyed, depending on whether he is just looking or waiting to cross the tracks.

In noisy evidence of this spectacle, class A No. 1225 is thundering up the Scioto Valley near Lucasville in June of 1957 with a solid 178 car train of company owned 70 ton hoppers, all loaded, for a total weight of 13,400 tons.

At left, above: As if to better the record, No. 1213 hits 50 an hour a few miles out of Portsmouth on the southbound haul with a record train of 213 cars! It is doubtful if the rear end crew ever saw the head end of this train once out of the Columbus yards.

Trios of black painted hood units now move the 175 car consists over the Baltimore & Ohio's three track diamond at Chillicothe where the smash of steel on steel was deafening. It is still an awesome sight but it was even more so in steam.

Above: Ranking as the world's most powerful reciprocating steam locomotive with a tractive effort, when operated in simple motion, of 190,000 pounds, the Norfolk & Western's class Y-6b 2-8-8-2 type is here giving evidence of its power.

The rock walled cut throwing back its exhaust in ear-splitting explosions, No. 2153 of this noted series is making 15 miles an hour on the long, hard climb up Christiansburg Mountain 20 miles west of Roanoke with 106 cars of westbound manifest.

Note the huge 39 inch diameter cylinders of the forward low pressure pair, which combined with the relatively low 58 inch driving wheels help to give this engine its tractive power rating.

Tromping over one of the spidery steel trestles which abound on the Norfolk & Western's Bluefield to Norton, Va., line, 2-8-8-2 No. 2088 is midway between St. Paul and Norton with 38 hoppers of a westward extra. No. 2088 is a Y-4 and one of the earliest of the N. & W.'s older Mallets to succumb to the effects of dieselization in the Pocahontas coal fields.

By 1958 dieselization on the Norfolk & Western had progressed to such an extent that only the most modern of steam motive power was still active. The smaller and older Mallet compounds, such as the Y-3 class 2-8-8-2's and Z-1b 2-6-6-2's along with the road's once numerous stable of 4-8-0's, had been sent to their retirement by the hooded invaders from La Grange.

As every follower of steam knows, the most modern of steam on the N. & W. meant 3 classes of motive power. These big three of the coal hauling road, were the 43 class A 2-6-6-4's, famous for the fast movement of 175 car coal trains over the more level reaches of the system, and the Y-6b 2-8-8-2's, operated either in simple or compound for use on the heavier grades in the Pocahontas coal regions.

The most famous of the three were, quite naturally, the 14 red and black streamlined J class 4-8-4's, used on the head end of virtually every main-line passenger haul. Modern they were too. The last three engines in the group were the 611-613, built as late as 1950. Utilizing integral cast

steel cylinders and frames, roller bearings throughout, lightweight alloy driving rods, and a completely automatic lubrication system, these engines were the ultimate in steam design. Operated on schedules allowing only a minimum of terminal servicing and turnaround time, several of these engines piled up an enviable mileage record, notably numbers 600 and 601, both of which in May 1954 rolled up a million miles of service.

In happier days, more specifically in 1953, the 605 is pictured above leading the 14 cars of No. 16, the eastbound *Cavalier*, around a curve at Eliston, Va. This is one of the quick turnaround schedules for which N. & W. motive power facilities are famous. The 605 will arrive at Roanoke at 12:30 p.m., cut off its train, and head for the large and modern engine servicing facilities at Shaffers Crossing, there to be washed, greased, have its fire cleaned, and at 2:45 p.m. be ready to leave the downtown station on the head end of No. 23, a westbound mail and express train.

One of the Grand Trunk Western's big lean and lanky Northerns, No. 6322, is boring down on the Pennsylvania's Logansport division crossing at Dwyer, Ind., at a flat 70 an hour with the 14 green and gold coaches and Pullmans of No. 20, the Montreal bound *Maple Leaf* on the first lap of its eastward haul.

The same run is pictured on yet another day, this time leaning into a curve a few miles east of Dwyer behind one of the rare breeds of streamlined steam engines that once flourished in competition with the diesel in the years of its infancy, this one No. 6410 of the Grand Trunk, resplendent in olive-green, black, and red and gold trim.

Above: Articulated No. 224 is engaged in an incessant conveyor belt flow of empties and loads as it wheels 168 empties out of the Proctor yards for the open pits at Hibbing over the ore stained rails of the D.M. & I.R.

Below: No. 611 of this great class of engines cools her heels on Cincinnati Union Terminal trackage waiting to take the *Powhatan Arrow* east on an early summer's morning in 1954.

At left: The ascending rails of the Missabe Road's long, heavy climb up from the Duluth lake front to the classification yards atop the bluffs at Proctor are white with finely ground sand from the passage of the ten-coupled engines used on this hill. One such behemoth, 2-10-4 No. 705, here with each exploding exhaust cannonading off the rock wall in the background, is fighting every inch of the way with 76 empty ore hoppers just off the ore docks.

In comparison with the noise of the 705's passing, the hollow rumble of the short wheel based ore cars is surprisingly silent. The road is fortunate that loads go downhill and empties return upgrade here. For even with the highest tractive force rating of any 2-10-4 ever constructed it takes all the 705 is capable of to hoist an 80 car train of empties up the 2% grade.

Above: Under a cloud studded Minnesota sky the Missabe Road's gargantuan limbed Yellowstone No. 221 is mothering 13,000 tons of raw, red earth down to the weighing scales at Proctor Yard, where after weighing and sorting, the 2-8-8-4's 170 odd car train will be dispatched to the holds of waiting Great Lakes steamers.

Above: With the tonnage ratings of the low slung K class 2-8-2's set at a conservative 252 tons for the 4% climb over Cumbres Pass east out of Chama, N. Mex., it takes more than one of the Rio Grande's low drivered, miniature steam giants to move any appreciable amount of freight over the slim gauge rails.

Just two tons under the safety limit, a Cumbres turn freight weighs in at 502 tons as two of the little Mikes pull and push 18 cars of narrow gauge freight on the upgrade out of Chama.

At Cumbres summit the lead engine will set the train out on a siding after which both engines will return light to Chama for another load, thus accumulating a more practical sized train for the trip downgrade to Alamosa on the following day.

At right, above: Same train a few miles further along is rounding Windy Point on the 4% grade just before reaching the summit.

Below: Their outside mounted counterweights describing arcs in the late afternoon sunlight, a pair of squat, fat-boilered K-36 Mikados, the 487 and 481, at Arboles, Colo., haul 48 cars of slim gauge freight on the last steam operated main line in the country, the Denver and Rio Grande Western.

With 22 active steam engines on the system roster the Denver and Rio Grande Western's narrow-gauge empire ranked as the largest steam operation in the country in the spring of 1959, an ironic turn of fate in view of the equipment's antiquity as compared with that of more modern gauge locomotives now nonexistent.

At left: A tandem of K-37 2-8-2's, the 497 and 493, are clipping along at a precarious 25 an hour on the dual gauge "speedway" across the flat San Luis Valley floor between Alamosa and Antonito, Colorado, with 48 cars of mixed three foot tonnage. At Antonito the lead engine will be placed in the middle of the train to equalize the pulling power of the two engines on the grade ahead over Cumbres Pass.

It is interesting to note that both of these engines, as did all of the K-37 class, started life as standard gauge 2-8-0's on the D. & R. G. W. but were converted to narrow gauge in the road's own shops in 1928.

Above: Easily handling a consist of 28 ancient, wooden planked gondolas, the 480 rounds the Horseshoe Curve near Maysville to head east for a half mile before again turning west and climbing ever upwards toward the snow speckled heights of 10,000 foot high Monarch Pass in the background.

The 480's easy progress is not due entirely to its own efforts however for another breed of the diminutive engines, No. 483, is shoving hard at the rear of the train.

Both engines are operating out of Salida on the limerock run in 1953.

Here on a bright Memorial Day in 1959 with nearly 400 camera toting fans filling every bit of passenger equipment left on the narrow gauge rails, including the bright green business car *Nomad* on the head end, the Rocky Mountain Railroad Club's special leaves Durango on the return portion of its three day circuit. Head end honors are being performed by a K-28 class outside frame Mikado No. 476 fitted with an impromptu diamond stack spark arrestor and sporting a fresh coat of black and silver paint for the occasion.

One of the most popular railfan treats in the past several years has been the Rocky Mountain Railroad Club's annually sponsored trip over the Denver and Rio Grande Western's remaining three foot gauge rails from Alamosa to Durango and Silverton and return. Featuring operations and scenery unparalleled anywhere in the land and pulled by an honest to goodness live steamer, the little trains' yearly goings bring a host of railfans and photographers from every corner of the United States and Canada.

Doubleheaded and smoking in a manner guaranteed to please the photographer, the 12 car Rocky Mountain Club special rolls up the light rails of the Silverton branch behind a tandem of K-28 class 2-8-2's a few miles out of Durango.

During the summer months this same equipment will make a regular daily round trip between Durango and Silverton, thus stealing honors as the only regularly carded passenger run behind steam power in the United States.

153

Above: While No. 480 labors on the head end, the 483 exhausts past the end of the three rail standard and narrow-gauge trackage out of Salida into the slim gauge world of its own.

Right, above: The Rio Grande's narrow-gauge Mike No. 480 exhausts smokily across the Arkansas River valley near Poncha Junction, Colo., while another 2-8-2 of the same breed, No. 483, works on the rear as together they pull and push a train of 56 wooden gondolas toward the reaches of Monarch Pass on the 3 foot gauge branch from Salida to the lime rock quarries at the summit.

Before beginning the final ascent, including the famous switchback at Maysville, the train will be divided into two lengths of 28 cars each, requiring two trips to complete the journey.

During the summer months two full trains a day are needed to keep the high grade lime rock moving to the Colorado Fuel & Iron Company smelters at Pueblo. The importance of this traffic is evidenced by the fact that in 1956 the Rio Grande standardized and dieselized the entire branch, thus ending another chapter in the history of Colorado's narrow gauges.

Right, below: Quite like dirty faced little rebels hiding from the wrath of their master, three of the Denver & Rio Grande Western's rotund little Mikados spend a quiet Sunday in the dark solitude of the Durango enginehouse. While the dawning of the following day will bring them attention galore as they are prepared for a double shotted run east, today only the occasional passage of the engine watchman and the roundhouse cat will interrupt their steamy slumber.

154

A pair of die-hards stare disconsolately at each other across the turntable pit at Madison, Ill., a few days before the end of steam operations on the Nickel Plate's western region in 1957.

Though not nearly so dominating on the landscape as coaling towers, but even more indispensable to the operation of every steam locomotive, whether oil or coal fired, was that trackside filling station, the water plug. Here a fireboy on the Rio Grande 3 foot gauge adds his weight to the spout as he fills the small, 6000 gallon tank of Mikado 498 as it prepares to leave the dual gauge trackage at Antonito, Colorado, for a night attack on the Cumbres Pass grade.

The sole remaining Pacific type in regular service on the entire Union Pacific system in the summer of 1955 was this product of the Harriman administration, No. 2888. Paired up with a 4-8-2 on the opposite end of the run, the 2888 was regularly hauling the now discontinued Cheyenne-Denver local No. 52. Provided with footboards in the event of local work to be done on the leisurely run, the 4-6-2 continued in this service until its retirement in late 1955. With its passing, the last of the fabled Harriman Pacifics with their generous stack, jutting smokebox, acutely tapered boiler, and generally speaking, jackrabbit appearance, joined a host of vanished notables.

Not all coaling towers were as impressive or did as thriving a business as the Union Pacific's all metal chute pictured at right at Cheyenne, Wyo., playing host to a multitude of big tanked power, but yet all were the scene of activities that were as characteristically a part of the era of steam as the locomotives themselves.

Union Pacific — Main Line West

Probably no other railroad endeared itself to the lovers of steam motive power during the early and middle 1950's as did the Union Pacific. Possessed of a heavy-duty, double tracked main line between Omaha and Ogden that carries a seasonal green fruit and wheat rush as no other road does, and operating only sufficient diesel motive power to cover normal periods of traffic, the road was compelled to keep on hand in operating condition a generous fleet of modern steam power to fall back on during these peak traffic periods.

In the slack winter months the backshops at Cheyenne were kept busy repairing this fleet of steam motive power. From mid July when the first trainload of green fruit from California dropped down Sherman Hill into Cheyenne until the last trainload of sugar beets was gathered in off the branches in eastern Colorado in late October, the skies over the double tracked iron were black from the exhausts of steam driven 4-6-6-4's and 4-8-4's rolling on mile a minute schedules with solid trains of dripping yellow P.F.E. refrigerators.

With an ever present number of high priority passenger hauls moving at a mile a minute pace over the main iron, Union Pacific dispatchers have to take advantage of every intervening space in their scheduling to keep the tonnage moving. Consequently, the 100-car blocks of sun bleached reefers tend to be dispatched from North Platte and Cheyenne in groups of four to five at a time on as little as 10 minutes headway. Once out of the yards on the main iron the big Alco built power moved with a vengance. More than one vacationing motorist has been tempted into keeping pace with one of these fast moving redballs on Highway 30 which parallels the U.P. iron across all of Nebraska and Wyoming only to awaken with a start to find the automobile speedometer registering well above the state speed limit.

Like the country they traversed, Union Pacific steam power was big. The mainstay of this reserve of power consisted of double stacked 4-8-4's, 4-6-6-4 Challengers, and 4-12-2's, plus the renowned 4-8-8-4 Big Boys with a sprinkling of veteran 2-8-2's and 2-10-2's coming alive at the height of the beet season in October. For the most part the U.P. confined its diesel power during the rush months to the divisions west of Laramie, Wyo., and between North Platte and Kansas City, while steam ruled unchallenged all across the 500 mile long Nebraska division. The yellow painted varnish of the *Fast Mail* and *Overland Limited* made time behind the 80-inch drivers of great, gray boilered 4-8-4's, while the green fruit and lumber rolled east behind the centipede tanks of Challengers and Big Boy articulateds and that most unusual of the unusual, the mighty three cylindered 9000 class 4-12-2's. These long boilered giants had made three cylindered talk across the rolling Nebraska hills for nearly thirty years before the increasing need for heavy repairs and the ever louder growl of 16-cylindered GP-9's began to still their distinctive exhaust. By the summer of 1955 they had become a rarity, and when the articulateds began to assemble in the Cheyenne yards for winter storage the few survivors were disposed of. They were conspicuous by their absence in the following years' operations.

The summer of 1956 and 1957 again saw the passage of steam power in quantities to warm the heart of every steam fan, but by late September of 1957 the show was about over. The arrival at that time of 100 new GP-9 road switcher units for service on the Nebraska division plus the increased use of the 4500 horsepower gas turbines, heretofore largely confined to operations west of Cheyenne, were enough to still the exhaust of all but a token force of steam. Alco built steam power may see duty in small quantities during the summer's rush yet but for those who have witnessed steam unchallenged on the main line west, the curtain had descended on the greatest show in the land. It was wonderful while it lasted.

Left: During a brief lull in the ever present rain squalls that cover the slopes of the Union Pacific's famed Sherman Hill in southeastern Wyoming, a 4-8-2 helper No. 7039 and a 4-8-4 road engine No. 832 are charging up the stormy 1.5% grade near Granite Canyon with the first section of No. 27, the *San Francisco Overland.* The 7039 and several other 4-8-2's of the 7000 series were regularly assigned to passenger train helper service over Sherman Hill until completion of the new Dale Cutoff, eliminating the grade and the consequent need for helper service.

Above: Challengers on the move! Two of the Union Pacific's fleet of 4-6-6-4 Challenger type articulateds are about to pass each other at speed near Thayer Junction, Wyo. The 3995 is headed for Green River with westbound empty reefers while the 3947 is thundering east at 60 an hour with 97 cars of oil and lumber. A drama of railroading seldom captured on film, the element of timing for such a photograph being far too delicate to predict. This one was purely accidental!

Above: A doubleheader of unusual proportions, a fat-stacked 2-8-2 No. 2223 with a hulking, elephant-eared 4-6-6-4 No. 3713 storming at its flanks, thunders up the west side of Sherman Hill near Hermosa, Wyo., with 90 cars of Union Pacific tonnage. Mikado types on the Overland Route in 1953, when this exposure was made, were few and far between. With the arrival of each new order of diesel power, the ranks of older steam power were thinned continuously, leaving only the road's most modern engines, Challengers, Big Boys, and 4-8-4's as reserve steam power. The few Mikados and Santa Fe types that remained only saw service seasonally on branch lines that became busy during the wheat and sugar beet harvest.

Right: Shades of an elephant eared 4-8-4! Sporting smoke deflectors similar to those used extensively on the 800 series Northerns, Challenger No. 3709 doublestack talks its way out of Rawlins Yard east toward Laramie. The sheet steel deflectors, copied after prevalent designs on European locomotives, were used extensively on the Union Pacific's 4-8-4's and a number of the Challenger 4-6-6-4's, especially after their proven usage on the wind-swept plains of Nebraska and Wyoming where the strong, prevailing northerly crosswinds made visibility for the head end crews nearly impossible in cold weather.

Right: A heavy accumulation of road grime and dust investing it with a ghostly glow under the inspection lights, Union Pacific 4-8-4 No. 836 waits to be called for a drag east out of Grand Island to Omaha. The 836 was one of approximately a dozen 800 class Northerns put into service between North Platte, Grand Island, and Council Bluffs during the seasonal rush in 1958.

This was the last service these fine locomotives saw, their days in passenger service finished and their use in freight service curtailed by the arrival of new turbine freight power. A wonderful parade of the finest in steam ended with their retirement.

Designed and constructed principally for passenger train service, the 800 series 4-8-4's of the Union Pacific, 45 in number, rarely stepped down from their princely assignments to power anything less than first class schedules. The assignment of diesel power to several varnish hauls besides the "City" streamliners did little to change this practice, the excess engines being put into storage rather than freight service. As each successive rush season passed, though, leaving a lesser number of regular freight power in operable condition, the big Northerns, fresh and ready from constant shopping and attention, were eyed with increasing interest. Finally in 1956 the full capabilities of these engines were unleashed in freight service. Confined

mainly to this service on the Eastern district of the Nebraska division between North Platte, Grand Island, and Omaha, the 800's repeatedly proved their worth. Accelerating out of the North Platte yards with either a 100 car drag or green fruit block, these high speed machines regularly ran the 137 mile distance to Grand Island nonstop in a little more than two hours. Vivid in this author's memory is the 808 charging full tilt out of Grand Island, westbound with the *Chicago-Denver Dispatch*, a daily hotshot given preferential treatment. Try as he might, the 808 was not to be approached. Vainly attempting to race ahead on the paralleling highway and thus gain a photograph of the fast moving train in the beautiful late afternoon light, the

driver floored the Chevy's gas pedal. All to no avail, the steady 65 to 70 an hour gait of the engine's 77 inch drivers proved insurmountable, the obstacles of traffic, though relatively light, and frequent restrictive speed limits only aided in widening the gap. Upon arrival at the North Platte enginehouse some two hours and 45 minutes later, the 808 was observed sighing peacefully, if not sarcastically, as it was being turned on the house table. One could almost imagine a sneer of contempt on its smoky face.

Waylaid the next day in a more leisurely fashion, the 808 is shown returning east with 102 cars of manifest some 20 miles east of North Platte at a flat 55 an hour. The 822 is making a grand showing as it hits the 60 mark

across the Nebraska countryside near Maxwell heading into the early morning sun with no less than 100 stock cars and reefers.

In the fall of 1958 roughly a dozen of these 4-8-4's were used in freight service again between North Platte and Council Bluffs for what appears to have been their last assignment.

It is a tribute to the designers and builders of these beautiful machines that there was very little that the Union Pacific could not ask and receive of them, be it wheeling a 100 car drag at the 60 mark or hitting a 100 an hour pace across all of Wyoming with the *Overland*. They were beautiful in action and stately in death.

Left: 9052, one of the last survivors of this once mighty race, its untended boiler flanks covered with a white crust of road grime and boiler compound, is hitting the summit of Archer grade a few miles east of Cheyenne, Wyo., in August of 1955 with an 85 car eastbound extra.

Above: Overshadowed in recent years by the arrival of the Challengers and Big Boys, but never to be forgotten by those who heard their offbeat thunder, the Overland Route's own Union Pacific type three cylinder 4-12-2's nonetheless rode into the sunset years of steam along with the finest in U.P. steam power.

The largest nonarticulated locomotive ever built with the longest driver wheelbase—some 30 feet, eight inches—ever designed, the 9000's were a natural outgrowth of the Union Pacific's ever present desire to move tonnage faster. Built by the U.P.'s favorite, American Locomotive Company, in the late 1920's, the 12-drivered behemoths soon outdistanced every engine type then on the road in economy, tonnage, and speed. Though Alco outshopped them

with a recommended speed restriction of 35 miles an hour, their 67 inch drivers and smooth riding qualities soon lured hogheads into rolling them at the 60 mark and above.

The sight of one of these long boilered monsters beating across the Nebraska prairie, its lengthy side rods flailing in a never ending arc to the tune of triple toned stack talk, is not easily forgotten. Invested with a string of superlatives, the 9000's were certainly unique and quite some engines.

The continuous punishment received during the traffic heavy war years and the succeeding seasonal rushes took their toll of the 9000's resources. Literally worn out and badly in need of major overhauls, they were the first of Union Pacific big power to succumb to the horde of yellow painted freight diesels. Of the original 88 locomotives all but 42 had been scrapped at the start of the traffic surge in 1955 and of these a mere two dozen were in operation. After nearly 30 years of continuous service on the rails of the Union Pacific from Omaha to Oregon, the last of their kind met the torch in spring of 1956, closing one of the most notable chapters of U.P. steam motive power.

Above: Across the rolling Wyoming uplands between Laramie and Green River, the Union Pacific's yellow-painted passenger hauls customarily roll at the 90 and 100 an hour mark on the heavily ballasted iron. No more than 10 miles out of Laramie on the westward haul, the 14 cars of No. 27 the *San Francisco Overland,* are rolling at 100 miles an hour behind the 80 inch drivers of smoke deflectored Northern No. 825. These big 4-8-4's of the 800 series were designed for and are capable of sustained speeds well above the 100 mark with the heaviest of U.P. passenger runs.

Below: Top man in the 800 series No. 844 is taking the 11 cars of 27, the *San Francisco Overland,* over the new cutoff between Cheyenne and Dale in the fall of 1958 in what is probably its last year.

Right: Running as the second section of No. 6, the eastbound *California Fast Mail,* a 15 car Boy Scout special tops the Archer Hill grade 10 miles east of Cheyenne, Wyo., at 40 an hour with 4-8-4 No. 822 on the smoky end.

168

UNION PACIFIC'S 3800 CLASS

With 200 newly arrived diesel units on the property to bolster an already growing fleet of such power, and with what appeared to be the heaviest fall traffic build-up yet just successfully handled the Union Pacific's operating management in late 1954 was convinced they were finished with steam. So firm was this belief that scores of the 3900 class Challengers were shoved into storage lines without further ado, water and steam lines undrained and little else done to aid in their preservation. The unexpected and spectacular nationwide business boom of the following year and its resultant record railway traffic volume soon showed the fallacy of this action. When the hastily stored 3900's were again turned to for relief the results of their too quick abolishment became evident. Undrained pipes and feedwater heaters had frozen and burst during the hard western winter, necessitating lengthy and extensive repairs before the engines could be of use.

An emergency call went out and from the storage tracks at Ogden and Pocatello the long silent and somewhat older

3800 class 4-6-6-4's, which had weathered the seasons in better shape than their unfortunate relations at Cheyenne, were inspected, fired up, and sent east to move tonnage across the Nebraska division. Thus in 1955 the 3800's suddenly appeared east of Cheyenne and there they remained until the end of steam on the Union Pacific.

Above: A clear order board beckoning at O'Fallon, Challenger No. 3823 is accelerating rapidly westward with a 117 car extra just off the North Platte hump.

At right: 4-6-6-4 No. 3803 darkens the early morning sky east of Cheyenne, Wyo., as it tops the short but steep Archer Hill grade out of the Cheyenne Valley with a 90 car extra.

170

Working against the elements of gradient and the perpetually buffeting wind on the uplands east of Cheyenne, the 9035 hurries an 87 car green fruit block up Archer Hill and on east to North Platte. Despite the prodigious fuel capacity of its 22 ton tanks, instances are recorded where a 9000 and other wheel arrangements for that matter have had to cut off their train and run light to the coaling stage at Pine Bluffs, Wyo., the constant uphill climb — and more importantly, the force of a 20 to 30 mile an hour cross wind against 100 billboard sized refrigerator cars — having sapped the fuel capacity to the danger point.

Its offbeat thunder sounding for fully 10 minutes before putting in an appearance, Union Pacific type No. 9080 races east on the Kansas division at Bonner Springs with 77 cars of Kansas City bound time freight No. 472.

At left: Rejoicing in its new found freedom of movement, temporary though it is, Challenger type No. 3805 hits close to 60 across Nebraska in the Platte River Valley near O'Fallon eastbound with 105 cars. In keeping with Union Pacific operating practice the 3805 is running close behind and ahead of several other eastbound freights, all moving in a block to take advantage of the lull in the passage of first class schedules.

Below: Bald faced 4-12-2 No. 9006 is beating its way west across the wind-swept eastern Wyoming uplands with 102 loads. The 9006 is one of eight 9000's rebuilt in the Omaha shops with an outside, double Walscheart valve gear arrangement in place of the original Gresley third cylinder motion on the pilot deck. Placement of the air pumps under the side running boards for better weight distribution accounts for the blank look forward.

Big Boy – Symbol of Survival

It seems only fitting that a special place of honor should be reserved in this assortment of photographs for that mightiest of the mighty, the Union Pacific's Big Boys. For years the largest and heaviest of iron horses to walk the earth, they have assumed yet another role in the history of steam motive power. They have become the very symbol of survival for steam. It is the confirmed belief of many railfans and steam historians alike that when the Big Boys pass out of existence the story of steam will have ended in the United States.

Constructed in 1941 and 1944 in groups of 10 and 15, respectively, to do battle with the heavy eastward grade through Weber Canyon in the Wasatch range east of Ogden, Utah, the 6000 horsepower machines proved their mettle not only in conquering this grade but once over it in their ability to hit a steady 60 to 65 an hour gait across the wind-swept high plains of Wyoming with a 100-car train of loaded reefers.

In more recent years, however, the division's points of Laramie and Cheyenne have become the home base for these giants. A circumstance of geology known as Sherman Hill stands squarely between these two points and forces the Union Pacific right of way to rise from an elevation of 6200 feet at Cheyenne to 8100 feet at the summit in front of the now razed depot at Sherman. It is this grade of 1.55% that brought the Big Boys east to do battle. The terms Sherman Hill and Big Boy have not only become synonymous but linked together became a Mecca for the serious minded student of steam.

During the late summer months when traffic over Sherman Hill was at its peak, railfans arrived with the regularity of clockwork from all corners of the continent to "lens" the beast in his lair. Probably no rail side location has been frequented by such a number of railfans as has the trackage just west of the Cheyenne Yard entrance. For it is here that one might experience the thrill of thrills, listen and gaze in awe as one of the great 4-8-8-4's charges out onto the main iron west shaking the girders of the Colorado and Southern overpass in its eager desire to do battle with the elements and gradient of Sherman Hill. It was a sight and sound not soon forgotten.

The Big Boys reigned supreme over the stormy desolation of Sherman Hill until the summer of 1957 when the Union Pacific began extensive use of the new gas turbines on the Hill. From a time when one could count the exhausts of as many as six 4000's climbing the grade out of Cheyenne, there came a day in September 1957 when not a single Big Boy was dispatched west out of the Cheyenne yards. This was not typical for the year, though, as Big Boys were in constant use during the peak traffic period, but it was the writing on the wall, even if one refused to read.

The year 1958 saw the last operations of the Big Boys. A total of 10 of the engines were called into service to lend a hand in moving Cheyenne-Laramie tonnage from late August through September. Needless to say, news of their activity brought the faithful from every corner of the nation for a last chance to savour their going. While the fortunate 10 saw nearly constant usage over the Hill the remaining members of the class sat silent in the Cheyenne enginehouse and on the storage tracks outside waiting for a call that would never come. Several of them were marked up as needing new tires and were thus unusable.

The 10 that saw action are to be commended, though, for their spectacular show once again on the Hill. It was grand and glorious and a little sad, knowing this was the last. For the symbol had fallen and the prophets were right, over the great forty-eight steam was gone. One of this great race should be enshrined for posterity at the foot of Sherman Hill.

This is it! The Mecca for all serious minded fans of steam. Probably the most photographed railroad location in the world, this is the west end of the Union Pacific's Cheyenne yards. Here, where the Colorado & Southern's overpass forms a perfect frame, is the beginning of Sherman Hill and from under the smoke stained trusses the world's mightiest big-voiced Big Boy storms forth to do battle with the immortal topography and elements.

When steam was rampant on the Hill during the late summer and fall rush, not a day passed but what a camera lens was not trained on this opening in the C. & S. embankment.

The thunderous passage of this biggest of the big as all 16 drivers dug in on the sanded rail could not be duplicated the world over, nor was one apt to forget the veritable hailstorm of cinders that fell hot and stinging from the volcanic doublestack.

Here are 594 tons of locomotive and tender shaking the earth and sky as the 4015 charges west in the grand march on Sherman Hill in August 1955. A thunderous anthem of steam in the grandest of halls.

Above: The 4001 and 4016 have teamed up above to hoist 102 cars of westward tonnage over the summit of Sherman and are here working wide open in an ear-splitting symphony of steam at work.

Below: Every standard tonnage train, passenger or freight, dare not move beyond the limits of the Cheyenne yards without proper assistance. This doubleheading over Sherman Hill accounted for the most spectacular and thunderous spectacle the Union Pacific could offer.

Heading an hour long parade of five eastbound freights, three steam powered with Big Boys and two behind diesel power, No. 4003 blasts upgrade under the signal bridge at Tie Siding, Wyo., with 74 cars of Cheyenne bound tonnage.

181

Above: No. 4018 and a more orthodox helper on the Hill, Challenger No. 3941, are digging in on the first few feet of grade just out of the Cheyenne yards.

Below: From front or rear there is no mistaking that Big Boy profile. The 4017 makes beautiful stack music west of Cheyenne in 1956 with an early morning extra.

At right: in steamier days on the Hill, July 1953 to be exact, a 4-6-6-4 Challenger No. 3956 and Big Boy No. 4019 team up to tackle the eastward ascending grade at Dale with 114 cars of stock, lumber and oil. The rugged desolation of the Sherman Mountains is quite apparent in this panoramic view.

In the below freezing air of a clear October morning the 4005 struggles upgrade over the new line at Speer, Wyo., with 101 cars whose cold journals and stiff grease do little to alleviate the articulated's work.

No. 4013, one of the ten Big Boys to see service in the fall of 1958, shatters the windswept solitude of the Sherman Mountains beating its way up from Laramie. The articulated's smoke had been visible towering over the heights for fully an hour before it hove into view at Hermosa around the curve in the distance.

After holding the momentum down while coasting through Hermosa Tunnel, the hogger of Big Boy No. 4017 has closed his brake valve, letting 4200 tons of locomotive and train hit 60 an hour on the 20 mile downgrade into Laramie, Wyo.

No. 4014 is westbound for Laramie with a 114 car drag whose box cars, flats, and reefers are still emerging from the west portal of Hermosa Tunnel in the distance. The eastbound tonnage of the 4013, already on the far side of the tunnel, adds to the backdrop in the deep cut.

Lingering only long enough in the terminals at Cheyenne and Laramie for necessary servicing and turnaround, the 4-8-8-4's passed over the summit of Sherman at such a frequency as to arouse suspicions as to whether the whole series of 25 locomotives were not in service after all.

Denuded of its original red and orange skirt and striping after its dethroning from the head end of such Southern Pacific flagships as the *Daylight* and the *Lark*, GS-4 Northern No. 4432 works its way upgrade through Santa Margarita Pass near San Luis Obispo, Calif., on a cool August morning in 1952 with mail and express train No. 72.

These famous 80 inch drivered Daylight type 4-8-4's which will best be remembered for their brilliant flash of red, orange, and black as they rolled across the California countryside with the Espee's best, spent their last years of service in a more somber and orthodox garb of black dulux, powering just such mail trains as No. 72 above and in their waning years on freight hauls on the coast line.

Espee Steam — Last in the Far West

The title for this one more look at the last of steam could hardly be more appropriate. Who else in the far west, and by far west we mean west of the Rockies in that fabled Gold Coast country of California, but the Southern Pacific could operate main-line steam to the last?

On railroads all across the continent it appeared that the rules for dieselization decreed that the western reaches of a system should succumb to the invader first. East of the Mississippi the Pennsylvania, New York Central, Baltimore & Ohio, and others abandoned steam on their western regions first, drawing their remaining external combustion power into ever tightening circles near convenient east end shops and headquarters. Farther west across the prairies and into the desert miles the Union Pacific, Santa Fe, and others followed suit, always dieselizing the farthest western divisions first.

With its headquarters and main steam repair shops and facilities located in California it was evident that if the Southern Pacific was to obey this established though unwritten rule, it must do likewise, though quite in reverse.

Accordingly, Espee dieselization started first in the desert country east of the California coastal area and spread west in complete opposition to current practices on the rest of the nation's dieselizing roads. This was indeed fortunate for the railfan population of California for in the interim before completion of the dieselizing process the grades and curves of the Coast and Valley divisions echoed happily to the sounds of big time Espee steam power, cab-forwards, helper engines, and GS class "Daylights." Even the escarpments of the Inyo Mountains in Owens Valley echoed, though substantially less in volume, to Espee steam power as a narrow-gauge 4-6-0 wandered across the lonely wastes on the still-in-steam Keeler branch.

It is entirely fitting and proper that the last of Espee steam should give its final performance in California. For no matter how far flung the Southern Pacific empire, and it does rate honors as operating more route miles than any other U.S. system, a Daylight engine or a cab forward gallavanting thru the orange groves or charging at Tehachapi seems entirely more appropriate than the same engine pictured elsewhere in Oregon or Texas. Espee steam power was as distinctly different as California itself. In keeping with this bold new land of the forty-niners radically new designs in place of age old concepts became the road's motive power trademark, as witnessed in the skyline casings and vivid colors of the renowned Daylight 4-8-4s, the same shrouding none the less startlingly applied to older pacifics and mountain types, plus of all engines, a freight mauling 2-8-8-4! Where else did a railroad have the audacity to operate its largest articulated power completely in reverse thus creating a completely new design which to the locomotive conscious typified California more than Hollywood itself. Yes—after a full century of Espee steam operations it was fitting that it end in the land of the Golden Gate.

Before all this came to an unhappy end in 1955 and 1956 let us take one more reminiscent look at the last of big and little power on the last steam operated divisions of the far reaching Southern Pacific.

TWO PHOTOS DONALD DUKE

Whether one approved or disapproved of their aesthetic values the Espee's famous cab-forward articulateds were without peer as the most notable and, understandably so, unusual designs of modern steam power to parade the high iron.

The placement of the operating crews' headquarters well ahead of the smoke exhaust and out from behind the long boiler which greatly obstructed the forward view in conventional articulateds, afforded the engineer and fireman a view of the track ahead hardly matched even by the blunt nosed diesels of EMD. This visual capacity was a special asset to operations in the snowsheds and on the abrupt curves in the High Sierra's of California and Nevada over whose grades these engines were designed to operate.

Indicative of the success to which the Espee management viewed this utilitarian arrangement of boiler and cab was the impressive total of 195 such machines put into service by the road since their origination in 1928. As if to bestow a further word of praise upon an already commendable machine the cab-forwards remained the ruling class of motive power on freight and passenger alike during the last years of Espee steam operations.

As shown here, two of the famous silver-chinned 4-8-8-2's, both class AC-11, team up to raise the dust from the roadbed with Los Angeles bound No. 58, the overnight *Owl* from San Francisco in September of 1951.

190

Not to be outdone during the three cylinder motive power craze of the 1920's that fathered such behemoths as the Union Pacific's 4-12-2 type the Southern Pacific Railway in 1925 and 1927 saw fit to order from the Alco works in Schenectady forty-nine long boilered three cylindered 4-10-2's. Although the Union Pacific had already put into service near identical engines of the same wheel arrange-

ment a year previous the Espee promptly dubbed their new wheel arrangement the Southern Pacific type and the name stuck.

No. 5012 of this series makes three cylinder stack talk on the upgrade through San Timateo Canyon at El Casco, Calif., in the waning years of operation.

TWO PHOTOS DONALD DUKE

The victor and the soon to be vanquished! While one of the Espee's growing fleet of diesel freight units idles in the passing track at Chatsworth, Calif., with a San Francisco bound time freight, a still resplendently painted GS-4 Northern No. 4455, like a mounted lancer charging full tilt at his sworn foe, barrels by on the main iron at 70 an hour with No. 98, the *Coast Daylight*.

Still stunningly bedecked in the striking livery of red, orange, silver, and black for which the Lima built GS class Northerns of the Southern Pacific were justifiably famous, No. 4450 picks its way through the slip switches of the Los Angeles Union Terminal throat tracks past a waiting terminal company diesel switcher with 18 cars of No. 99, the *Coast Daylight*. The accompanying blanket of early morning fog, or to use the more publicized version, "smog," only aids in heightening the impression of this most colorful, and to California railfans, revered, steam run.

A Southern Pacific AC class 2-8-8-4 No. 3801 rolls 127 empty box and flat cars of freight No. 550 along the shore of Pyramid Lake at Sutcliffe, Nev., over the Espee's single track, freight only line between Fernley, Nev., and Klamath Falls, Ore.

To the local train crews the line is known as the Modoc, a moniker no doubt derived from the tribe of Indians of the same name which once inhabited the region. The line is of great importance to the Espee's scheme of things, for over it a great amount of southern Oregon and northern California lumber moves to eastern markets. The lumber moves over the Modoc to the small yards at Fernley, several miles east of the main division point of Sparks, from where it is moved east over the main iron to Ogden and beyond.

No. 3801 is a locomotive notable in at least two respects. Outside of the skyline dome casing applied to the top of its boiler, similar to the casings on the more famous GS-4 Daylights, the 2-8-8-4 is one of a group of 10 such locomotives constructed with the more conventional arrangement of cab and pilot deck as opposed to the large fleet of cab-ahead type articulateds for which the Southern Pacific is singularly famous. The 3801 was designed originally for use as a coal burner for operations on the division between Tucumcari and El Paso where the lack of tunnels and numerous curvatures did not necessitate the practical yet aesthetically questionable cab-forward design.

The complete conversion to diesel operations of this New Mexico division in 1953 moved the AC-3's to the Modoc division where along with a large group of cab-forwards they operated until that line's eventual dieselization in 1956 forced their retirement.

At left is, to the operating department of the Espee, one of the more conventional cab-forward 4-8-8-2's, No. 4159, at Wadsworth, Nev., with scheduled freight No. 559 and 142 cars of lumber on the Modoc. Both of these exposures were made in July of 1954.

194

The unusual in perspective is afforded here by another of the Southern Pacific's cab-forwards No. 4181 as it pulls from the passing track onto the main iron of the coast line at Santa Margarita, Calif., with an eastbound or Los Angeles bound time freight, first No. 920, whose mixed consist of reefers and high cars is being carefully scrutinized by the hogger while in this advantageous position.

Although the Espee's rails lie physically in a south-north direction between Los Angeles and San Francisco, the operating timecard lists all trains as either eastbound or westbound, L.A. being to the east while San Francisco is to the west.

DONALD DUKE

THE KEELER BRANCH

Important enough in the company's economic eye to warrant the purchase of a specially constructed three foot gauge internal combustion unit with which to continue operations, the Southern Pacific's Keeler branch in southern California's Owens Valley lived on in direct defiance to statements that narrow gauge today is an anachronism. While narrow-gauge lines by score have passed into the non-existent state in the last twenty years leaving only a vestige of the vast Colorado network of 3 foot rail spacings and none whatsoever east of the Rockies, this seemingly incongruous segment of the mighty Espee empire operated daily in the shadow of the Sierra Nevada until early 1960.

With a profitable enough freight traffic in minerals and livestock to insure its existence for several years to come, the Keeler branch is one of few common carrier narrow-gauge lines to make the switch from steam to diesel operations in lieu of the usual complete abandonment, a fact aided to some extent by the solvency of its standard gauge owner.

Although the single diesel unit did preserve the line and its intriguing operations, for the orthodox lover of steam, however, its real charm was in the three little Baldwin Ten-wheelers which comprised the motive power during the last few years of the branch's operations in steam until October of 1954.

These three remaining remnants of the old Nevada-California-Oregon Railway, acquired from that line when the S.P. standard gauged its rails, were numbers 8, 9, and 18. Possessed of a quaint turtle backed tender and an endearing look they captivated the hearts of short line steam lovers everywhere.

Though numbers 8 and 18 were donated to the State of Nevada and to Inyo County, Calif., respectively, No. 9 remained on the roster and saw service on an average of twice a year when No. 1, the 45 ton diesel electric replacement was indisposed due to inspections and repairs.

196

At left, below: A white faced No. 18 eases away from the moss-covered water tank at Laws, Calif., northern extremity of the Espee's 70 mile long Keeler branch, with 22 sun-bleached, narrow-gauged boxcars on the return trip to the yards at Owenyo.

Due to the abundant and consistent leakage from the ancient water tower the area is resplendent under a covering of lush, thick grass.

Above: No. 18 is "horsed around" by three men on the 1883 vintage Gallows type turntable at Laws. Rank and seniority both go by the wayside here as the whole head end crew pitches in to help turn the venerable steamer.

One of the last remaining hand operated Gallows type tables in the land, it helped give the Owens Valley line its flavor of old time railroading.

DONALD DUKE

PHOTOS COURTESY DONALD DUKE

AT THE ROCK OF CAJON

Memories of steam in California could hardly be complete without a look back at the last of it on what is undoubtedly the most celebrated piece of railroad topography in the west—Cajon Pass. What Horseshoe Curve and its accompanying grades are to the Pennsylvania Railroad in the east so Cajon Pass is to the joint operations of the Santa Fe and Union Pacific in the far west. This double tracked right of way over a natural saddle in the San Bernardino mountains acts as a funnel through which all traffic carried by these two major transcontinental systems must pass between the glittering valley floor at Los Angeles and the far distant eastern terminals.

Assuredly not the highest point reached by the rails of either railroad, yet considerably steeper in gradient than Union Pacific's Sherman Hill and quite on a par with the Santa Fe's highest elevating climb at Raton Pass in New Mexico the right of way over Cajon is inclined at a power sapping 2 to 3 per cent on the eastward climb while a more lenient though still limiting 1.5 per cent exists on the lengthier westward approach. The necessary usage of heavy motive power dispatched in multiples to move ton-

nage over such a steep climb plus an abundance of flange gripping curves set amidst some of the most beautiful backdrop scenery in the west served to make Cajon Pass a favorite haunt of rail photographers in steam's heyday.

Above: The Santa Fe's 80 inch drivered 4-8-4 No. 2923 is going it alone on the less sharply ascending westward grade west of Victorville at sunup of a chilly April morning with No. 23, the *Grand Canyon Limited.*

At right: Here at one of the Pass' most remembered and publicized locations, at the Rock of Cajon Pass, two Mr. "Bigs" of the Union Pacific, a 4-8-4 road engine No. 829, and a one time three cylindered 4-10-2 helper No. 5093 render a pluperfect reason for the Cajon's popularity in the days of steam as they hoist the now discontinued *Los Angeles Limited,* train No. 2 on the U.P., up the 2.2% to the tune of ricocheting exhausts. Note that the 829 does not yet have the elephant eared smoke deflectors applied to it in this pre-1950 photo.

A Baltimore & Ohio graphite faced Pacific No. 5206 smokes across the rolling southern Indiana farmland near North Vernon with a three car Louisville to Cincinnati local. The passenger hauls on this run remained with steam long after all others on the system had been committed to diesel power.

This photograph was made just days before the Louisville Line trains were converted to diesel, ending all steam hauled passenger runs on the B. & O. The date of this exposure was August, 1956. The 5206 was last known to be residing quietly in the Washington, Ind., enginehouse, its future uncertain.

"Mountains on the Flatlands"

Although the Union Pacific's main line across Nebraska unquestionably witnessed the greatest passage of steam power west of the Mississippi in the early 1950's, the Chicago division of the Baltimore & Ohio across Ohio and Indiana could lay claim to this distinction east of the big river. From smoke filled yards at the Willard, Ohio, junction point of the Akron and Chicago divisions, the Timesaver freights and steel trains rolled west on short headway behind the spoke drivers of home built and ex B.&M. 4-8-2's, with an occasional President class Pacific thrown in for good measure.

While continuing with a policy of eventual complete dieselization, the B.&O. concentrated on dieselizing the rest of its system first while confining its steam power to the lines west of Newcastle, thus gaining the advantage of maintaining steam facilities on only one major division.

Scheduling allowed the largest bulk of eastbound tonnage to arrive at the Willard Yard during the morning hours while the heavy westbound movement began in the afternoon, thus permitting favorable light during the heaviest traffic hours, made such locations as "J" tower at the west yard entrance and the Pennsylvania crossing at Attica Junction, some five miles west, a rail photographer's veritable paradise. Only the occasional blast of an air horn on the internal-combustion units of the *Royal Blue* and *Columbian* added a discordant note to the otherwise symphonic melody of chime whistle playing atop tapered boiler courses.

While a President class 4-6-2 did appear frequently doubleheading with a 4-8-2, the majority of tonnage pounded across the diamonds at Fostoria and Deshler behind the B.&O.'s own T-3 class 4-8-2's, a group of Mountain types built at the Mt. Clare shops in 1943 using boilers from an outmoded group of Mikados. In addition to this group of 4-8-2's the road added the 13 class T-4 engines of the same wheel arrangement purchased from the Boston & Maine at the same time the T-3's were under construction.

Across the flat, gradeless topography of northern Ohio and Indiana these engines proved once again the recognized theory that on a gradeless, water-level route a 4-8-2 was ideal for moving freight fast. Entrusted with the system's hottest freight run, the highly touted Timesaver service runs, whose delay for one minute would raise eyebrows in the deepest carpeted halls of B.&O. officialdom, the fast stepping 4-8-2's came up out of the sag west of Attica Junction and hit the Pennsylvania crossing at 50 to 60 per, rocking the merchandise cars in their race east.

By mid 1950, however, a condition came to exist which, to the layman, is not often thought of as contributing to steam's downfall. With nary a single steam locomotive having been built for commercial use in nearly 10 years, those concerns supplying the major builders with accessories and parts had long since ceased business or turned to other sources of revenue. Thus the B.&O., like others before it, found its maintenance forces needing grates, feedwater heater parts, valve gear linkages, and other steam engine appurtenances formerly supplied by outside firms. In desperation the road turned to the only solution possible, a solution that was self destructive—cannibalism of its own remaining steam power. Those engines with the least amount of boiler time remaining or most in need of repairs were selected as the first victims and stripped of parts necessary to keep healthier relatives alive. Two to three engines were parked in the Willard enginehouse at all times waiting to give a transfusion, so to speak, to ailing brethren.

No mathematical formula is necessary for one to realize the eventual end of such a program. Self destruction of the entire steam roster was the only and inevitable end. Although this had not been fully accomplished at the time of this writing, and the year 1957 had seen a constant parade of 4-8-2's west from Willard, the lack of business in 1958 helped to wipe steam from the double track iron.

Generous shopping and maintenance on the part of the system's enginehouse forces kept the T-3's and T-4's in fine physical and aesthetic shape but the odds were too great; lack of parts and lack of business both helped finish the day for Baltimore and Ohio steam power, Chicago division power included. The parade of Mountains in an otherwise diesel infested area, however, was quite a treat for several years.

Under a gray, leaden sky on the page opposite the Baltimore & Ohio's No. 297, the Detroit Steel run, rolls west out of Willard, Ohio sporting a doubleheader of 4-8-2's. In the lead is No. 5590, a class T-3 built in the B. & O.'s own shops at Mt. Clare, and the road engine is No. 5651, a T-4 acquired from the Boston & Maine.

Above: One hundred empty hoppers get a fast and smoky ride through College Grove, Ohio behind a smoke-belching 4-8-2 No. 5559. The train is headed south on the B. & O.'s Toledo division for Cincinnati where the empties will be taken into the Kentucky coal fields by the Louisville & Nashville. No. 5559 is another Mt. Clare built engine utilizing boilers from scrapped World War I 2-8-2's and new 70 inch driving wheels. The road built 87 such machines between 1943 and 1947. Their sharply angled boiler taper just ahead of the steam dome comes from the use of shorter Mikado boilers.

Above: Another pair of Baltimore & Ohio Mountains find the weather sullen and gray as they pound out of the ordered confusion of Willard yard on a westbound extra. Both of these engines are class T-3 sporting new numbers in the 700 series under the road's steam motive power renumbering scheme of 1957.

At left: Taken from the tower window at the Pennsylvania's crossing at Siam, Ohio, the Baltimore & Ohio's eastbound dispatch freight No. 84 is hitting a flat 60 an hour behind the pounding drivers of T-4 class Mountain No. 5651. A near miss was almost recorded here due to the untimely passage of a westbound peddler freight behind a

2-8-2 moments before the redball freight came into focus. The caboose of the receding freight is still visible just out of interference range.

The 5651 is a secondhand acquisition from the Boston & Maine, secured through the B. & O.'s purchase of 13 such engines in 1947. Renumbered in the road's roster as series 5651 to 5002, the lower numbered half of the series saw service mainly on the Chicago division west of Willard, Ohio, while the 5655 and up normally were assigned to the lines east of Willard on the Akron and Pittsburgh divisions. A high drivered 4-8-2 with 75 inch wheels, the T-4 class was right at home wheeling freight or passenger on these reasonably level divisions of the B. & O.

With the diesel powered, number one train on the St. Louis division, the *National Limited*, following close on their markers, Baltimore & Ohio Pacifics No. 5208 and 5206, the former equipped with a sheet metal pilot not at all in keeping with the conventional B. & O. spoke models, are streaking across the American bottoms near Caseyville, Ill., like the proverbial bats out of hell with a 14 car westward military extra.

Judging from the frequency of their passage, the operating management of the Baltimore & Ohio had little if any aversion against doubleheading its freight runs over the Chicago division. The frequency of traffic on this important main line plus an abundant supply of steam power released from other recently dieselized districts may account in part for this practice. Whatever the reason, double shotted freight runs were quite the vogue in the summer of 1956 and 57.

Here in August of the earlier year mentioned a tandem of B. & O. steamers are romping east over the main iron at 60 an hour near Siam, Ohio, with 111 cars of Timesaver freight No. 294. The road engine is a conventional freight locomotive No. 5559, a class T-3 4-8-2, while the lead engine is one of the road's famous President class Pacifics once assigned to only the finest of the Capitol Route's passenger runs. Painted an eye appealing shade of royal blue and with a stride equal to its 80 inch drive wheels, this was a rare treat to find on the head end of a freight haul. The 5309, however, and a sister President class No. 5306 finished out their days of service doubleheading freight runs over the Chicago division.

207

Smoke in the Red River Valley

Down in the Red River valley of central Kentucky nestles a community so small its existence is not even recognized on the official state map. Its existence could hardly be ignored by the Louisville & Nashville Railroad, however, for it was at this point during the days of steam that the 100-car trains of Harlan County coal bound for Cincinnati and the Great Lakes were forced to halt while reinforcements were added to whatever motive power had brought the coal up from the division point at Corbin, Ky. For north of Ford lie 21 miles of tortuously curving, 1% ascending grade, covered for the most part by smoke lined tunnels that compose the northward ruling grade on the road's Cincinnati-Atlanta main line.

The helper engines drifted down light from the small engine terminal at Winchester at the top of the grade to lie in wait in the siding perched along the river's edge at Ford until a northbound drag burst out of the bore that tunnels through the hogback ridge on the south side of the river. After waiting for the seemingly endless string of red hoppers to roll by and grind to a halt, the helper would emerge from its lair to snuggle noisily up to the little red hack at the end of the drag.

Up ahead along the river's edge the lead engines would uncouple, take on water pumped directly from the river below, then recouple to their train and await a signal from the rear. The helper engine whistled off and at the exact instant all three engines surged forward and the fight was on. The sight and sound was tremendous, for in the narrow river valley surrounded on all sides by high ridges the whistles and exhausts cannonaded back and forth in an ear-splitting crescendo.

When the rear engine blasted by and disappeared into the first tunnel a scant 200 yards away, one would think the grade was conquered and the battle nearly won. Come upon the trio of motive power three miles further on, though, and they were to be found fighting for every inch of distance. Coal is heavy stuff and it takes a lot of power to lift 8000 tons of it up this hill.

Winchester is the top of the grade and here the lead helper and the pusher engine were dropped, leaving a single 2-8-4 to roll the tonnage the remaining 98 level miles to the receiving yards at DeCoursey.

The practice of dropping the helper engines at Winchester invariably resulted in a surplus of idle motive power overcrowding the small engine terminal. When this occurred the next southbound drag of empties was stopped and the extra helper engines added to the head end for a return trip to the division point at Corbin. Beside giving rise to many doubleheaders, this frequently created that rarity of motive power operation, a tripleheader in action!

This wondrous spectacle of steam and steel has been absent from the Red River valley for some three years. The little community of Ford awakens now only to the guttural growl of black sided GP-9's moaning upgrade with the still present coal drags. The only evidence of the mighty M-1 2-8-4's that made the valley an arena of ricocheting whistles and steam talk are the cinders lying ankle deep where once stood the damp water plug.

This picture story really begins on page 208. The photographer appears to be the center of attention from the rear end crew as M-1 No. 1967 shoves hard to keep the slack bunched on 101 cars of Kentucky coal moving out of Ford. The crowning plume of smoke and steam ascending into the crisp autumn air is indicative of the thunderous ovation existing at the moment as the 2-8-4's stack exhaust is bounced from one side of the river to the other among the surrounding palisades of rock.

The echoed scream of its whistle and that of two similar Berkshires on the head end as they signaled their movements to one another in getting under way in this canyon of echoes was indeed a sound for which posterity will be the poorer.

The grade is lessening. Despite the plume of smoke on the horizon the two M-1's on the head end are finding the going considerably easier. The exhaust of Berkshire No. 1967, pushing hard at the rear of the 110 car coal drag pictured above, is quickening as the grade begins to level out across the rolling Kentucky fields. In a few moments the summit at Winchester will be reached and the 1967 will drop off to wait its next pusher assignment out of Ford.

Louisville & Nashville's M-1 class 2-8-4's have the distinction of being the most expensive engines of this wheel arrangement ever constructed, their designers embodying every improvement and notable feature known to the steam locomotive builders.

The passage of 136 coal laden hoppers having only just cleared the bore of exhaust gases left by the two locomotives on the head end, 2-8-4 No. 1974 is about to be swallowed up by the first tunnel out of Ford, Ky., as it shoves hard against the drawbar of the northbound drag's cinder covered caboose.

The head end crew of the Louisville & Nashville's double-headed 2-8-4's No. 1959 and 1978 who at the present moment are intently watching the photographer, will shortly bang shut the cab windows and wrap bandannas about their faces as they slam into one of the many tunnels on the L. & N.'s Cincinnati division. The pair of M-1's are leading 101 cars of Harlan County coal out of the Red River gorge and up the grade between Ford and Winchester, Ky.

An overabundance of helper engines used on the northward ascending grade between Ford and Winchester, Ky., has resulted in the ultimate in this spectacle of steam in action: a triple-shotted 136 car empty coal hopper drag descending the grade near Flanigan station with M-1 Berkshires No. 1950, 1980, and 1978 on the smoky end. All three engines will return to the Corbin, Ky., yards where after servicing they will return north, either single or doubleheaded with tonnage trains.

Tripleheading was a frequent occurrence on this division where common practice was to doublehead the northbound tonnage trains between Corbin and Winchester, dropping the extra engine at the latter point. After two or three such northbound drags had passed, the small engine terminal at Winchester would be crowded to capacity giving rise to such sights as that pictured.

At left: Their tumultuous exhausts reverberating among the hogback ridges bordering the Red River at this point, three of the Louisville & Nashville's M-1 class 2-8-4's are working hard as they get under way with 113 cars on the northbound ruling grade out of Ford, Ky. Nos. 1961 and 1991 are on the head end while No. 1974, whose smoke is visible over the ridge in the background, is shoving hard on the rear.

Despite mountain grades and big tonnage the L. & N. never indulged in a ten-coupled engine, much less an articulated. Until the arrival of the M-1's in 1942, the road spread the heavy work amongst its U.S.R.A. heavy Mikado types. Reports have it the management really wanted a dual service 4-8-4 but the South Louisville shop couldn't accommodate the longer frame so a 2-8-4 was selected as a compromise and to this date there have been no regrets.

Rumor has it the management was still desiring a 4-8-4 when the diesels and their lower axle loadings appeared on the scene.

When the M-1's were brand new, several were placed in a passenger pool between Cincinnati and Corbin, Ky., handling war swollen passenger traffic. Their performance in this service proved that with their 69 inch disc drivers and roller bearings they could turn a mean wheel.

Above: Santa Fe No. 5013 approaches the B.&O. crossing trailing company hoppers.

ALONG THE
Atchison, Topeka & Ohio

Before regaling in what may appear to be a typographical error in the heading above the reader is asked to peruse the following text carefully, after which he will no doubt agree the heading is more correct for this sequence of photographs.

The Pennsylvania Railroad brought many a railfan into the flatlands of northern Ohio in the summer of 1956 when it leased from the Santa Fe 12 of that road's 5012 class 2-10-4's for use in hauling coal from the Columbus yards to the lake port at Sandusky. These engines operated throughout the summer and helped to bolster the already thinned ranks of the Pennsy's own J-1 class 2-10-4's normally used in this service.

A brief but interesting comparison of the two engines from an operating crew's standpoint, obtained from the head end crew of Santa Fe No. 5016 as they waited in the passing track for a meet north of Siam, Ohio, might be of interest here. It was the undeniable opinion of the veteran hogger of this crew that the Pennsylvania engine could start a heavier train than the Santa Fe engine but once in motion the Santa Fe locomotive could keep the train rolling at a faster rate. A comparison of the driver size on the two locomotives, the Pennsylvania J-1a having 69-inch wheels as opposed to the Santa Fe's 74 inches, plus a higher horsepower rating for the latter engine makes this comparison quite obvious. The grizzled boomer fireman, who claimed to have fired engines from Pocatello to Port Jervis, was more enthused over the extra amount of seatbox time the Santa Fe engines afforded due to using oil in place of coal for fuel, than he was in either engine's ability to move tonnage.

As stated previously, the branch of the Pennsylvania on which the Santa Fe engines saw service is a seasonably used line. The rails lie in almost a straight line between Columbus and Sandusky and their sole purpose is to move coal north to the docks at Sandusky and ore south. During the months when the Great Lakes are open to navigation, the long trains of coal laden hoppers roll north in a seemingly endless parade. When the lakes freeze over, though, this traffic comes to a standstill. The only train to brush aside the rust on the railheads during the long winter months is an every other day local freight. As a result the rails are not too lovingly tended and in the spring receive only enough attention to insure the passage of the coal drags. Consequently the passage of a 10,000 ton coal train behind one of these enormous 2-10-4's at a 30 to 40 mile an hour gait is apt to be quite unnerving.

A note of interest concerning the biggest of Santa Fe power here on lease: in the Pennsylvania's Columbus engine terminal the A.T.&S.F. behemoths had to be turned on a wye since their combined engine and tender length of 123 feet was too much for the existing turntable!

Summed up, it was a welcome treat for the railfan and well deserved chance for a fine engine to breathe smoke and steam once again.

At left: Lacking prior knowledge of the situation or operating territories of the railroads involved a layman viewer would be hard put to identify this train. One hundred and one black Norfolk & Western hopper cars, hauled by a monstrous 2-10-4 with Santa Fe in five foot letters across its tank and ending with a faded red Pennsylvania Railroad caboose, are easing up to the Baltimore & Ohio's crossing at Siam, Ohio. After a wait of several minutes for the interlocking to clear, the Santa Fe leased power took up slack and surged forward to hammer the double track diamond at an ever increasing rate.

A few moments after the caboose at the end of the 5012's drag had bounced over the crossing gaps, the 5034 which had been waiting in the passing track a half mile north of the crossing came thundering south with a mile of empty foreign line hoppers swaying precariously behind on the ill maintained iron.

Above: One of the Pennsylvania's own J-1a class 2-10-4's charges up to the B.&O. crossing at Siam, Ohio with a mile of hoppers swaying behind.

LEASED POWER

In the early summer of 1956 the Pennsylvania Railroad found itself lacking in sufficient diesel-electric motive power to move the increasingly heavy tonnage of the season. By this time, however, its once great fleet of steam motive power had been reduced through repeated scrappings and lack of repairs to such an extent that little of its reserve power could be manned to meet the needs. If the traffic was to move there was no alternative left but to lease the stored power of another road.

Thus it was, as pictured elsewhere in this volume, Santa Fe 2-10-4's appeared on coal trains in Ohio while further east leased Reading Railroad class T-1 4-8-4's came to life and pounded the rails of the Susquehanna division between Enola Yard and Williamsport, Pa.

The 70 inch Box Pok drivers of Reading No. 2114 are doing just that as the hefty mannered Northern rolls south near Dalmatia, Pa., with 88 cars of Pennsylvania Railroad symbol freight EC-2.

On another day yet another Reading 4-8-4, this one No. 2119 crosses the famous Susquehanna River bridge at Rockville, Pa., again with symbol freight EC-2 trailing behind.

There are some schools of thought who believe that the Pennsylvania would not have been so quick to dieselize had it forsaken the idiosyncracies of duplex drive power for a more conventional 4-8-4 of this design.

M-4 No. 6312 rolls 132 empties south near Vermont, Illinois. One of the distinguishing features of these locomotives is the large, square tender with its outside fish-belly underframe. In keeping with traditional Burlington policy the engine is wiped clean of road grime and freshly painted where needed, a trait of the "Q" in steam which was kept up to the end.

At right: Hauling its consist in a somewhat unorthodox arrangement, a 1910 vintage 2-6-2 Prairie type of the "Q" is making the Beardstown division's local peddler run between Litchfield and Beardstown in 1951.

Branch Line to the Coal Fields

The three track main line west out of Chicago and the single track branches meandering across Iowa and Nebraska are as familiar to fans of the Burlington Route as its famous 0-5a Northerns and Zephyr streamliners. Not so familiar, though, judging from the lack of publicity and photographs, is the Q's Beardstown division rails.

This division has its beginning in the sprawling classification yards at Galesburg, Ill., where so many Burlington divisions originate. The single track rails reach into the coal fields of southern Illinois sending offshoots into every coal mine within reach before continuing on to cross the Ohio River on its own bridge. The line terminates at Paducah, Ky., a state not generally known to be reached by Burlington rails.

It is the coal field operations, however, that mainly account for the line's existence and for the use of the system's heaviest power over its rails.

Although operated in quantity on nearly every segment of the Burlington Route, the appearance of a 2-8-2 on the Beardstown division was indeed a rarity. When steam ruled the division it was in the form of long boilered, graphite faced 2-10-2's and 2-10-4's. The coal drags were long and heavy and it took plenty of power to keep them moving across even the level Illinois prairies. The M-2 class of 2-10-2's built in 1914 were the mainstay of motive power on the division until the advent of the newer and heavier M-4 2-10-4's built for the Q in 1927. Until the assumption of operations by diesel power in mid 1950, the M-4's and M-2's worked jointly to move the coal north to the main line at Galesburg.

During the war years when traffic was heavy and copies of "19" orders were picked up at every station calling for a meet with an opposing drag at the next passing track, it was not uncommon for the 16-hour "hog law" to catch the crews halfway on the 130 miles between Centralia and Beardstown.

When the daily passenger run on the Burlington Route's Beardstown division departed from Beardstown in the early morning hours, it consisted solely of one diesel powered R.P.O. coach-combine, No. 9844. Not far along the way, however, its diesel unit went into a decline and stubbornly refused all attempts at physical therapy. At length all hope of revival was abandoned and a call for aid was sounded. Help arrived in the form of an aged but active Burlington Pacific No. 2931 which, kept stored in the Beardstown enginehouse for just such an occasion, was promptly substituted for the ailing diesel unit and train No. 11 was once again in motion.

Here, running some three hours late on the return trip north, the ailing unit hides its face shamefully behind the tender of the high stacked, seemingly haughty veteran steamer at Smithboro, Ill.

Long the standard in motive power on the Beardstown division a class M-2 2-10-2 No. 6101 plods north thru Litchfield, Ill., at the precarious rate of twenty miles an hour. An even one hundred loads of southern Illinois bituminous are trudging stubbornly behind. During the second World War when fuel for the fires of war industry was in an ever increasing demand the M-2s worked the branch line exclusively and seldom were the prairie rails silent from the bellowing exhaust of their passage. A World War I vintage machine, the M-2s were the typical in the low drivered drag freight power in predominance at the turn of the century.

The Bashful Berkshires

Should a judging be held to determine which of the Illinois Central's square domed steam locomotive classes were to have the dubious honor of being the least photographed and publicized, most assuredly the 8000 class 2-8-4's would carry the field. Seldom is this breed of engine pictured in a publication and yet at its birth it was at once the object of rapt attention and publicity in every railroad circle. No. 8049 of this series was none other than Lima Locomotive Works once famous No. 1, the original superpower design freight locomotive that not only brought about steam locomotive design changes that were used in every engine built since but sired identical 2-8-4 designs on half a dozen roads.

As pictured here, though, the famous Lima design bore only scant resemblance to its original design. During the I.C.'s profitable campaign in the late 1930's to rebuild and standardize its steam motive power to meet specific needs the 2-8-4's lost their most distinguishing characteristic—the Elesco feedwater heater that hung over the brow of the smokebox door. With the removal of this Lima trademark and the placement of the headlight in the center of the smokebox door, along with the removal of that seemingly arch enemy of I.C. power, the air compressor shields on the pilot beam, the engine assumed the standardized design of all Illinois Central power.

Designed primarily for rugged, mountainous service on heavy grades it is interesting to note that the entire group of 50 engines was assigned to service on the nearly gradeless, curveless, Edgewood Cutoff line between Bluford, Ill., and Fulton, Ky. It is this single track line constructed in 1929 to relieve the pressure on the double track main line further west that sees the bulk of the tremendous north-south freight traffic of the Illinois Central, and until their demise in late 1956 it was the 8000's that performed the majority of work on the division.

As of this writing all of the 8000's have long since gone the way of all steam locomotives and now only the growl of V-16 diesels can be heard on the Edgewood Cutoff. In the days that were, however, the 2-8-4's ruled the roost.

No. 8028 is here about to enter tunnel No. 1 on the Edgewood Cutoff at Abbott, Ill., with 101 company cars of Kentucky Coal. The Berkshire has waited in the passing track for two closely following banana specials to run around it and is now following them north, although at not quite the same pace.

This division was the exclusive territory of the 8000 class 2-8-4's, and only an occasional Mountain class entered their domain. They were the first of the heavy steam power to disappear completely from the Illinois Central's roster, retired all at one time by EMD road switchers.

Originally built by Lima in 1926 following the original A-1 superpower design the 50 Berkshires of the I.C. were rebuilt as class 8000 during the I.C.'s steam modernization program in 1937.

The smoke of its exhaust had been visible over the 40 mile tangent stretching south from Bluford, Ill., for fully an hour in the still evening air before Illinois Central Berkshire No. 8036 rolled into view. The Big Mike, as this type is known in I.C. enginehouses, is heading north with 97 cars of Kentucky coal on the freight only Edgewood Cutoff line through southern Illinois.

This single track division extending from the yards and engine terminal at Bluford to Fulton, Ky., was the exclusive territory of the 8000 class 2-8-4's. Nowhere else on the Illinois Central system could they be found. Only an occasional Mountain type entered this domain, usually to power the nightly first class merchandiser MS-1. This supremacy was also their undoing, for they were the first class of heavy steam power to disappear completely from the I.C.'s roster. As the management dieselized the Edge-

wood Cutoff with EMD road switchers, the 8000's were retired, one and all immediately.

As originally built by Lima in 1926 following the noted original A-1 superpower design by that company, the 50 Berkshires of the I.C. bore a considerably different appearance from that shown above. Most notable was the Elesco feedwater heater hung in front of the smokebox door following, in true Lima tradition, the design of the 2-8-4's and 2-10-4's built at that time for the Boston & Albany and Texas & Pacific. Sporting numbers in the 7000 series and in use all over the northern districts of the system, the engines emerged from the Paducah, Ky., shops after extensive rebuilding during the I.C.'s steam modernization program in 1937 as class 8000. It was during this rebuilding that the engines lost their original wooden pilots and that heavy-hung Elesco heater, the management at this time having come to look upon such appliances as entirely superfluous.

It is entirely conceivable that one reason for the lack of photographs of the 8000's in action is the near inaccessibility of good vantage points on the Edgewood Cutoff line. The 40 miles of tangent south of Bluford, mentioned before, combined with a high growth of weeds bordering a single track line in rugged, undeveloped countryside, does not lend itself well to fine photography. To secure good vantage points in the southern part of the state where the three tunnels and their accompanying deep cuts are located takes time and lots of footwork.

This shot of the 8015 entailed a nerve wracking walk across a towering timber trestle that included little provision for safety in the event of a train suddenly appearing around a distant curve. The 2-8-4 is climbing a ridge in the Ozark foothills of southern Illinois with a 93 car northbound redball.

Above: Sixteen 80 inch drive wheels bit hard into sanded rail as doubleheaded 4-8-4's swing into action out of Borie, Wyo., with the *San Francisco Overland,* now some two hours late after the road engine, No. 833, stalled on the grade between Otto and Granite Canyon and had to call for help.

She Fell Down on the Hill

September 1, 1957 was a black day for the Union Pacific's 833. Normally with a single 4-8-4 on the head end, No. 27, the *San Francisco Overland,* would have proceeded over the easier graded new line over Sherman Hill but on this particular day a flock of westbound freights crawling up the Hill on the new line forced a change in routing. As the 833 pulled from beneath the umbrella sheds of the Cheyenne depot, the dispatcher gave the operator at tower "A" orders to route No. 27 onto track 1, over the old line, the original route over Sherman Hill with the 1.55% westward ruling grade where doubleheaded 4-8-4's were the rule on anything over 11 cars. No. 27 had 13 cars this day, all heavyweight equipment, and a strong headwind to contend with.

The 833 showed her stuff but the odds were too great. She made a grand showing charging out of Cheyenne and on up to Borie, but between Borie and Granite Canyon the going gets rough. The cadence of her exhaust slackened gradually until the pauses between stack exhausts were long enough to cause apprehension in the minds of the onlookers. Finally at Otto, high on the hill, the 833 faltered once, twice, a third time and then died. The goggled, sweating and fuming hogger backed up spreading sand on the rail as he retreated, paused to build up steam and then tried again, all to no avail. Retreat was sounded and the 833 and No. 27 eased slowly back down the Hill. She tied up at Borie to await help.

Dubious aid arrived in the form of two carloads of official brass. Mutterings were heard concerning mechanical difficulty on the 833. Bona fide help soon arrived, however, in the form of the 837. After much popping of safety valves and throbbing of air pumps, the 837 whistled in her flagman and announced to the crowd of officials and waiting railfans that she was ready to tackle the grade in earnest.

Finally, more than two hours since the 833 had charged out of the Cheyenne depot, No. 27 was again in motion. There was power to spare this time and with eight pairs of 80-inch drivers digging into the sanded rail the big 4-8-4's surged out of Borie and up the grade with a vengeance. There was no pause at Otto this time. The 4-8-4's walked through Granite Canyon at 40 per and by the time they rolled through Buford the racing railfans on the paralleling highway were hard put to keep pace.

No Hollywood movie star ever had a greater show of attention than the 833 and 837 as they charged out of Borie. No less than 12 different cameras held by a like number of railfans were trained on their performance. This was indicative of the popularity among railfans of the Union Pacific during the seasonal height of its steam operations each summer and fall.

Above and at right: The battle is nearly won as the 4-8-4 tandem charges into Buford at 50 an hour, just four miles from the summit. Once again Union Pacific steam and steel have challenged the Hill and won. In a mad rage of indignation the skies over Sherman turned a threatening black. Indeed, as the markers of No. 27 disappeared over the battlements at Sherman, it was as though the impudent challenger had been swallowed by the darkening elements.

At right, below: The speed is 35 an hour now as the 837 and 833 swing wide on the curve into Granite Canyon. There is no sign of stalling now as both Northerns work wide open, double-stack exhausts slapping into the surrounding granite covered heights in thunderous applause.

A Portfolio of Steam

At right: A Great Northern 2-10-2 No. 2186 works out of Moorhead, Minn., under a magnificent plume of smoke and steam in a subfreezing temperature in October of 1956.

TWO PHOTOS FRED SANKOFF

A true collector's item! The Northern Alberta's No. 1, the overnight passenger from Edmonton to once roaring Dawson Creek, replete with head end equipment, first class coaches and heavyweight sleepers rolls up the main iron in the grand manner a few miles out of Edmonton under a sky blackened by the rolling oil smoke exhaust of blue-painted Pacific No. 161. No. 1's consist includes equipment not only from its own ranks but from the connecting Canadian Pacific and Canadian National also. The 161 itself was once on the Canadian Pacific roster as No. 2563.

The recording of this passage of the N.A.R.'s finest is indeed fortunate at this time in view of management's decision to replace the entire train at the time of the road's complete dieselization with a self-propelled R.D.C. type car on a day run. This will be a regrettable loss indeed to the railfan fraternity.

Featured above is the Northern Alberta's own 2-10-0 Decapod type No. 52 rolling ponderously across the prairie
north of Carbondale, Alberta with the daily local on the
300 mile Edmonton-Waterways branch. Listed in the time-
table as No. 7 with coaches only, its consist is as unusual
a concoction as may be found in this day of streamlined,
air-conditioned equipment. The two head end cars are
wartime troop sleepers now serving as baggage cars, while
the center storage car is a truss rod braced piece apparent-
ly of older origin than its steel sheathed sides intimate. The
second car from the rear is a combination caboose-coach
with a bay window jutting from its wooden sides for the
convenience of the crew while finally on the tail end is
the orthodox and advertised steel coach.

237

TWO PHOTOS FRED SANKOFF

On loan to the Canadian National during the peak traffic
period of 1956 a 4-8-4 of the Ontario Northland Railway
No. 1102 ramrods a Canadian National freight extra
through Oriole, Ontario enroute to Grevenhurst under a
snow threatening February sky.

Covered with a sparkling new coat of locomotive black and sporting the impressive new coat of arms of the Canadian National done in red and gold on her tender flanks, Pacific No. 5101 is just out of the Stratford, Ontario shops working her way back to assignment at Port Arthur by assisting Mikado No. 3505 up the grade through Todmarden, Ont., with a 36 car company coal drag.

Though carrying the white flags of an extra, the Colorado & Southern's little graphite faced 4-6-0 No. 909, wallowing in a sea of grass as it passes through a meadow a few miles out of Cheyenne, Wyo., is pulling the 12 freight cars and ancient, faded red, wooden combination baggage-mail and passenger car of train No. 160, a triweekly mixed operating between Cheyenne and Sterling, Nebr.

Since this photograph was taken in 1952, the Ten-wheeler's duties have been assumed by a gargoyle faced diesel powered coach and R.P.O. combine whose passing leaves the Wyoming meadows in a fog of acrid blue exhaust, not a healthy improvement over the sentimental notions of the 909's going, to say the least.

At the time of this photograph the Cotton Belt was possessed of no more than two passenger service diesel units, both 2000 horsepower Alco products, and both in service on the overnight St. Louis to Dallas *Morning Star Limited*. Thus with both units in service on the north and south hauls simultaneously, a shopping or failure of either unit automatically meant the use of one of the road's stocky little 4-6-0 Ten-wheelers, kept spic and span in the Illmo, Mo., and Pine Bluff, Ark., enginehouses for just such an occasion.

It was such an occasion on October 15, 1951, that caused the five car consist of No. 6, complete with the silver roofed private observation car *Ranger* on the tail end, to go charging up the Mississippi River bridge approach at East St. Louis, Ill., behind the "cheesecake" disc drivers of No. 664, proud and shining in the early morning sun, to this photographer's delight.

At left: The 30-odd cars of assorted freight coupled to the red and silver trimmed tank of the Louisville & Nashville's streamstyled 4-6-2 No. 275 are a far cry from the swank, first class passenger hauls the engine was accustomed to commanding in plushier days. Such notables as the *Pan-American* and the *Dixie Limited* were regularly accelerated across the southland behind its chime whistle and rapid exhaust. Like so many name trains in this day of dusk for the steam engine, they now cover their schedules behind the grunt and growl of the fume spuming diesel, leaving the 275 to fill out its life on less advertised tasks.

Having once stirred the public imagination with the radically styled sheathing applied to it during the heyday of steam streamlining in the 1930's, the veteran Pacific, actually built in 1924, here performs the workaday task of rolling a St. Louis division freight extra out of the East St. Louis yards on a windy March day in 1952.

A fearsome looking doubleheader of the Baltimore & Ohio's massive S-1 class 2-10-2's No. 6157 and No. 6199 roar down the Toledo division's single track iron near Wapakoneta, Ohio, with 135 empty hoppers headed south for the rails of the Louisville & Nashville and the coal fields of Kentucky.

Since no engine changes were involved on the 200 mile Cincinnati-Toledo run, only two of the streamlined Pacifics were in actual operation on the *Cincinnatian* at any one time, the remaining two held in reserve or in use out of Cincinnati on Louisville, Ky., bound runs. Here, some 20 miles south of the junction point of North Vernon, the 5303 is literally "streaking" across the rolling Indiana countryside at the head end of No. 57, an overnight Detroit-Louisville run.

PRESIDENTS IN STREAMLINE DRESS

There have been many and varied attempts at streamlining a conventional steam locomotive with results both good and bad. It is this photographer's confirmed opinion, however, that none achieved the aesthetic success gained by the Baltimore & Ohio in streamstyling four of its original 1927 built President class Pacifics for service on the *Cincinnatian*. Rebuilt at the Mt. Clare shops in 1946 to handle this train over its then assigned run between Washington, D.C., and Cincinnati, Ohio, the changes wrought in their design were more than aesthetic. All four locomotives, Nos. 5301-5304, were also given cast steel engine beds, roller bearings throughout, intertrain telephones, and large capacity tenders.

When the *Cincinnatian* was reassigned to the Detroit-Toledo-Cincinnati haul some few years later, the stream-styled, blue painted 4-6-2's went along also, in spite of the fact that Electro-Motive power had already captured every other name train on the system. At the head end of the *Cincinnatian* they stayed, however, resisting dieselization until the fall of 1956 when they were finally retired in favor of the growlers.

Their bullet nosed profile racing across the Ohio flat-lands with this sightliest of B.&O. streamliners was a beautiful occasion indeed, as witness above the 5301 in full dress accelerating south out of Lima, Ohio, with the train's nine car consist on a Memorial Day evening in 1955.

After spending the night slumbering quietly behind the little three stall enginehouse nestled in the West Virginia mountains at Page, the Virginian Railroad's low drivered Pacific No. 211 rolls grandly out of town at the first light of dawn with the road's daily scheduled varnish No. 14 on the leisurely nine hour trip to Roanoke.

With the small coal mining community of Page as its westernmost terminus, it is small wonder that revenue passenger service on the little train steadily diminished until the run was discontinued completely a few years after this trip was photographed in August 1953.

Hurrying south near Adolph, Minn., is probably the most rarely photographed passenger haul within the boundaries of the United States. Listed on the operating timecard as Nos. 1 and 2, it is the Duluth, Missabe & Iron Range's daily varnish between Duluth and Hibbing, Minn., making a complete round trip between sunrise and sunset.

Powered by one of the rare examples of Missabe Road passenger engines, a carefully groomed 4-6-2 No. 401, the train's four car consist is complete with baggage car, coaches, and a brightly polished olive green solarium-observation on the rear that sports an illuminated tail gate banner proclaiming the run to be the *Arrowhead Resorter*. No main-line transcontinental haul could boast of a more impressive end to its complement.

Scarcely a year after this exposure was made in August 1952 the little run remained but a memory, having been abandoned completely while the remaining passenger haul from Duluth to Virginia on the Iron Range Road had been converted to a diesel powered R.D.C. car.

Running on the wrong main while bypassing a freight working up the long grade out of the Kaw River valley behind it, the Santa Fe's big 84 inch drivered Hudson No. 3465 charges west at 50 an hour near Olathe, Kan., with the 12 cars of No. 19, the *California Fast Mail.*

A pair of sprightly Canadian National class K 4-6-2's, the 5595 and 5578, are hitting it up on the straightaway into Toronto, Ontario, with a company coal train of 36 Illinois Central hoppers.

A late March sun glinting off its newly applied coat of blue and white enamel, Wabash Hudson No. 701 is fresh from the backshops at Decatur as it accelerates the six cars of No. 1, the *Detroit-St. Louis Limited,* into stride after a brief stop at the Litchfield, Ill., station.

No. 701 is one of seven such engines constructed in the Wabash's own shops at Decatur, Ill., between 1943 and 1947 utilizing boilers from a class of World War I vintage three cylinder 2-8-2's.

Before their creation the heaviest passenger power on the road was the 660-675 class of light but fleet Pacifics whose 73 inch drivers when coupled ahead of the six car *Bluebird* could turn in a speed record to equal that of any higher drivered engine.

The need for more tractive effort to handle longer and heavier passenger trains spurred the construction of the 700 series Hudsons. Veteran hoggers, however, who had commanded both classes of motive power and were familiar with the bite of the lower drivered 4-6-2's when starting a train, complained that the Hudson's 80 inch drivers made it a bit slippery at starting but once in motion was the fastest thing on rails!

The management, nevertheless, was impressed enough by the performance of this newest of motive power as to plan for the construction of several more such machines. These plans died a-borning though, when the rapid shift to diesel electric power began in earnest in 1950.

Like so many before it, this noble line of steam power spent its last years of existence in the quiet and solitude of the abandoned roundhouse at Decatur, staring blankly through the glass windows waiting for an assignment that would never come.

Sweeping down into the Ohio River valley at close to 75
an hour behind Hudson No. 5387, the New York Central's
Cincinnati Mercury is only 10 minutes and 12 miles out of
its southern terminus on the Cleveland-Cincinnati run.

Excepting the heavyweight, standard design mail storage cars on the head end its consist is the original lightweight, four wheel trucked, light gray painted equipment
of the Chicago-Detroit *Mercury* which made headlines behind a radically streamlined 4-6-2 with illuminated running gear in the streamline conscious 1930's.

But for the modern electric head lamp and steel slat pilot of Pacific No. 154, the year could well be 1900 instead of 1953, for with its consist of truss-rod braced wooden coaches and plush observation car, replete with brass railing and oil lit markers, the Clinchfield's lone passenger haul, No. 38, rolling into the Great Smokies south of Erwin, Tenn., could pass for a train from a yesteryear of wooden equipment, hand fired engines, and railroading in the grand manner.

Despite the modernities of electric generator and cross-compound air compressor, the little 4-6-2 at its head end only helps to complete the picture since its brightly polished boiler jacket and brass rimmed number plate are reminiscent of the general trend of steam motive power maintenance at the turn of the century. This is a far cry from the prediesel hit and miss steam maintenance policies of mid 1950.

At left: About to fade into the shadows of a hazy October afternoon sun, the Missouri Pacific's 4-8-4 No. 2208 is bellowing across the wooded Missouri hills near Grays Summit with 125 empty stock and refrigerator cars of extra west No. 2208.

Above: Thundering west under a rolling cloud of oil smoke, the Rock Island's 4-8-2 No. 4049 is on the head end of a 16 car military extra at Muncie, Kan. The train is running over the joint Rock Island-Union Pacific trackage between Kansas City and Topeka, Kan.

A few minutes before and New York Central 4-8-2 No. 2943 had a mile of freight train rolling behind it on the St. Louis division. During this lapse of time, though, the L-2d class *Mohawk* pulled into the receiving yards at Mitchell, Ill., dropped its train, and now after picking up the rear end crew is hightailing it down the main iron for the East St. Louis enginehouse some 15 miles distant.

The small capacity of the inbound yards at East St. Louis and the belt line connections at Mitchell make this a not too uncommon operation on the Big Four Route, especially should the consist be westbound empties moving at the train dispatcher's discretion.

No. 2943 is one of the early groups of Mohawks, and for a number of years after its construction in 1929 carried the number 6643 and the name of its parent road—the Chicago, Cleveland, Cincinnati and St. Louis—before that road's absorption into the New York Central System.

Assigned to the Missouri Pacific's subsidiary, International-Great Northern, and seldom seen outside the boundaries of Texas, this 2-8-4 Berkshire No. 1121 is a long way from I-GN trackage as it pounds north over the Illinois division toward the Dupo classification yards with a 73 car extra.

Reason for the appearance so far from home base of the 1121 and four other oil burning 2-8-4's of the Mo Pac's BK-63 class was a nationwide strike of coal miners called on such short notice in the winter of 1950, when this photograph was taken, as to catch many railroads short of fuel for coal fired locomotives. The Mo Pac was fortunate in that all power assigned to the I-GN had been converted to oil burners and the road thus was able to operate without interruption through the fuel fasting period by utilizing this power where needed.

Although the Missouri Pacific's motive power stable is well known for its conversion of 25 Lima built superpower Berkshires into dual service Northerns in 1940, the road's ownership of these five I-GN Berkshires is not generally known, judging from the amount, or lack of, attention accorded them in previous publications dealing with railroad motive power. In view of their extremely handsome appearance and kingly proportions, there seems little justification for this ignorance of their existence unless it be a case of a face lost in the crowd.

With practically every roundhouse on the system crowded with Pacifics, Mountains, Northerns, and even aged Ten-wheelers vying with one another in the matter of which is the better looking, one would be hard put to single out any one particular class of Mo Pac engine as the best looking of the lot. Indeed, though many roads had larger locomotives or one particularly famous engine type, for variety and sheer good looks in steam motive power, the Missouri Pacific was second to none.

At left: One of the few tributes that may be credited to the United States Railroad Administration created during World War I was the design of several sightly and well proportioned classes of steam motive power, which were distributed to roads throughout the country. It is a further tribute to the desginers of these engines to find many of these U.S.R.A. types still in active service long after more modern and heavier power had been replaced by the diesel electric.

Here in December 1952, on the crooked, sharply descending grade at Dutch Hollow, Ill., that drops the Louisville & Nashville's single track line off the high river bluffs to the river bottom classification yards at East St. Louis, the hogger of U.S.R.A. Mikado No. 1533 is cracking the whip with the 38 cars of time freight No. 58, the *Bullet,* at close to 55 an hour.

Above: It is 6:00 p.m. to the minute and the Missouri Pacific's Texas-St. Louis fast mail, is on the advertised as the big 4-6-2 No. 6618 on the head end, charges across the Arkansas River lift bridge at North Little Rock, Ark., and accelerates the consist of 18 storage mail, express, and R.P.O. cars northward under a waning sun.

At left: Indispensable to the operation of every steam locomotive, whether oil or coal fired, was that trackside filling station, the water plug. Whether it be the Sylvania Central's 19th century 4-6-0 siphoning bream filled water from a lineside creek or a roller-bearinged Big Boy taking a monstrous draw at the Harriman plug the need and action were the same; an insatiable thirst that was both a pleasure to witness from the point of its admiring fans and scourge to operations as viewed by the operating department. Indeed, it was this thirst itself that aided and abetted steam's eventual downfall. Witness the age old stance of the fireboy as he waits patiently while a veritable river of water is discharged into the 22,000 gallon tank of a B.&O. EM-1 articulated.

Below: Another U.S.R.A. 2-8-2, this one beefed up with an air compressor on the pilot deck and a large capacity, 6 wheel trucked tank, thunders north along the banks of the Ohio River at Coroapolis, Pa., on the heavily trafficked four-track main of the Pittsburgh & Lake Erie with 42 cars of steeltown tonnage.

The pasage of heavy drivered Mountains and Northerns had been continuous on the Canadian National's double tracked main line west from Toronto to Hamilton Junction on this particular day in August 1955. With nearly a score of Boy Scout passenger extras added to the usual heavy schedule of regularly carded runs, it was nearly midday before a lull in the parade of heavy power occurred.

The pause was just long enough, though, for Canadian Pacific Ten wheeler No. 820 to put in a seemingly incongruous appearance as it trundled 12 cars of peddler freight west over the leased trackage.

An eight car extra of storage mail and express westbound out of Chicago has paused at the Galesburg, Ill., station just long enough for servicing and a fresh change of motive power. After arriving from the east behind 4-6-4 Hudson No. 3003, the train is now being accelerated rapidly out of town on the double track main behind a freshly shopped O-5a Northern No. 5600 its tank emblazoned with a five foot square red and gold trademark of the Burlington Route.

The railroads, the locations, and even the wheel arrangements differ, but the stance, the situation, and the time are the same. It is the summer of 1959 and throughout the land the sounds of steam are few and far between. What power did attempt a small comeback was quickly silenced by the repercussions of that year's steel strike. Over all the land the last-ditch holdouts surrendered unconditionally and waited in their entrenchments for the final judgment.

In the enginehouse at Lorain, Ohio, the once reigning monarchs of the Baltimore & Ohio's steam roster, the mighty EM-1's sat staring coldly out onto a landscape they had little chance of trodding again.

Some 2000 miles west a pair of even mightier steam go-liaths repeated the pose. Union Pacific's 4007 and 4022 slept soundly in their silent quarters at Laramie, Wyo., oblivious to the arrogant jeers of multiple unit "Geeps" and howling turbines heading east to do battle with the unchanging topography of Sherman Hill.

The symbol of survival sat silent. A chapter of history has been brought to a close. To the lover of steam there is but one consolation; to have lived in the era when steam was king!

Index

Page

Akron, Canton & Youngstown
Locomotives:
#406, 2-8-2...........................110

Arkansas Railroad.........................98
Locomotives:
#411, 2-6-2...........................105

Atchison, Topeka & Santa Fe...............71, 217
Locomotives:
#2910, 4-8-4........................... 77
#2923, 4-8-4...........................198
#3461, 4-6-4........................... 78
#3465, 4-6-4...........................248
#3752, 4-8-4........................... 74
#3761, 4-8-4........................... 70
#3770, 4-8-4........................... 74
#3782, 4-8-4........................... 76
#3927, 2-10-2........................72, 73
#5012, 2-10-4...................73, 218, 221
#5013, 2-10-4...........................216
#5014, 2-10-4........................... 75
#5030, 2-10-4........................72, 73
#5034, 2-10-4...........................218

Augusta Railroad........................98, 100
Locomotives:
#300, 2-6-0........................100, 101

Baltimore & Ohio Railroad...............117, 201
Locomotives:
#655, class EM-1, 2-8-8-4........116, 118, 120
#661, class EM-1, 2-8-8-4................ 263
#662, class EM-1, 2-8-8-4................156
#672, class EM-1, 2-8-8-4............121, 260
#706, class T-3, 4-8-2...................205
#708, class T-3, 4-8-2...................205
#5206, class P-5a, 4-6-2............200, 206
#5208, class P-5a, 4-6-2...............206
#5301, class P-7d, 4-6-2...............245
#5303, class P-7d, 4-6-2...............244
#5309, class P-7c, 4-6-2...............207

#5590, class T-3, 4-8-2..................202
#5559, class T-3, 4-8-2.............203, 207
#5651, class T-4, 4-8-2.............202, 204
#6120, class S-1, 2-10-2.................123
#6157, class S-1a, 2-10-2................243
#6199, class S-1a, 2-10-2................243
#7604, class EM-1, 2-8-8-4..............122
#7605, Class EM-1, 2-8-8-4..............121
#7606, class EM-1, 2-8-8-4..............119

Canadian National Railway....................132
Locomotives:
#3505, Class S-1-g, 2-8-2................239
#5098, class J-4-c, 4-6-2 (on DW&P)....... 40
#5101, class J-4-d, 4-6-2................239
#5578, class K-3, 4-6-2.................249
#5595, class K-3, 4-6-2.................249

Canadian Pacific............................. 83
Locomotives:
#852, class D-10e, 4-6-0.................261
#2916, class F-1a, 4-4-4................. 84
#5387, class P-2f, 2-8-2................. 85
#5931, class T-1b, 2-10-4.............82, 83
#5935, class T-1b, 2-10-4................ 85

Central of Georgia
Locomotives:
#415, 4-6-2.............................107

Central of Vermont
Locomotives:
#466, class N5a, 2-8-0.................. 13

Chesapeake & Ohio Railway................... 79
Locomotives:
#610, class J-3a, 4-8-4.................. 79
#1506, class H-6, 2-6-6-2................ 81
#1624, class H-8, 2-6-6-6................ 78
#2707, class K-4, 2-8-4.................. 80

Page

Chicago, Burlington & Quincy..............125, 223
  Locomotives:
    #2197, class R-5, 2-6-2....................223
    #2931, class S-2a, 4-6-2..................224
    #4002, class S-4a, 4-6-4..................126
    #5509, class O-4, 2-8-2...................129
    #5600, class O-5a, 4-8-4..................262
    #5624, class O-5a, 4-8-4..................128
    #5629, class O-5a, 4-8-4..................127
    #5632, class O-5a, 4-8-4..................124
    #6101, class M-2, 2-10-2..................225
    #6312, class M-4a, 2-10-4.................222

Chicago & Illinois Midland................... 9
  Locomotives:
    #502, class A-1, 4-4-0.................... 55
    #655, class G-3, 2-10-2................... 52
    #700, class H-1, 2-10-2................... 53
    #701, class H-1, 2-10-2................... 53

Chicago, Milwaukee, St. Paul & Pacific
  Locomotives:
    #215, class S-2, 4-8-4.................... 36

Chicago & Northwestern
  Locomotives:
    #1648, class E, 4-6-2..................... 33
    #3027, class H-1, 4-8-4................... 31
    #4002, class E-4, 4-6-4................... 33

Chicago, Rock Island & Pacific............... 9
  Locomotives:
    #4049, class M-50A, 4-8-2.................255
    #5114, class R-67B, 4-8-4................. 34
    #5117, class R-67B, 4-8-4..............34, 35

Chicago, St. Paul, Minneapolis & Omaha
  Locomotives:
    #424, 2-8-2............................... 32

Clinchfield Railroad
  Locomotives:
    #154, 4-6-2...............................253

Colorado & Southern
  Locomotives:
    #909, 4-6-0...............................240

Delaware & Hudson
  Locomotives:
    #1507, class J, 4-6-6-4................... 14

Page

Denver & Rio Grande Western..................133
  Locomotives:
    #473, class K-28, 2-8-2...................153
    #476, class K-28, 2-8-2..............152, 153
    #480, class K-36, 2-8-2..............151, 155
    #481, class K-36, 2-8-2..............149, 155
    #483, class K-36, 2-8-2...................154
    #486, class K-36, 2-8-2...................155
    #487, class K-36, 2-8-2..............149, 155
    #489, class K-36, 2-8-2...................155
    #493, class K-37, 2-8-2...................150
    #497, class K-37, 2-8-2..............149, 150
    #498, class K-37, 2-8-2.........148, 149, 157

Detroit, Toledo & Ironton
  Locomotives:
    #811, 2-8-2............................... 30

Duluth, Missabe & Iron Range.................132
  Locomotives:
    #221, class M-3, 2-8-8-4..................147
    #224, class M-3, 2-8-8-4..................145
    #401, class P, 4-6-2......................247
    #607, class S-7, 0-10-2...................139
    #705, class E-4, 2-10-4...................146

Duluth, Winnipeg & Pacific
  Locomotives:
    #2460, class N-2-a, 2-8-0,................ 40
    #5098, class J-4-c, 4-6-2, leased Canadian
      National engine......................... 40

East Broad Top Railroad...................... 97
  Locomotives:
    #16, 2-8-2................................ 98

Ferdinand Railway
  Locomotives:
    #3, 4-4-0................................. 96

Galesburg & Great Eastern
  Locomotives:
    #4, 2-8-0.................................102

Grand Trunk Western..........................132
  Locomotives:
    #6322, class U-3-b 4-8-4..................144
    #6410, class U-4-b, 4-8-4.................144

Great Northern Railway....................... 57
  Locomotives:
    #2053, class R-2, 2-8-8-2..............58, 59
    #2186, class Q-2, 2-10-2..............56, 235
    #2525, class P-2, 4-8-2................... 60
    #2551, class S-1, 4-8-4................... 61
    #3388, class O-8, 2-8-2................... 61

266

Page

Illinois Central...........................87, 227
Locomotives:
#1257, 2-8-2.............................. 90
#2417, 4-8-2.............................. 90
#2525, 4-8-2.............................. 89
#2526, 4-8-2.............................. 86
#2527, 4-8-2.............................. 89
#2600, 4-8-2.............................. 91
#2704, 2-10-2............................. 91
#2743, 2-10-2............................. 88
#8015, 2-8-4.............................229
#8028, 2-8-4.............................226
#8036, 2-8-4.............................228

Interstate Railroad
Locomotives:
#6, 2-8-0................................109

Kansas City Southern
Locomotives:
#220, class L, 2-10-2..................... 28

Lehigh Valley
Locomotives:
#5126, class T-3, 4-8-4.................. 17

Litchfield & Madison
Locomotives:
#161, 2-8-2.............................110

Louisville, New Albany & Corydon
Locomotives:
#9, 4-4-0............................... 99

Louisville & Nashville....................209
Locomotives:
#275, class K-5, 4-6-2...................242
#1533, class J-3, 2-8-2..................258
#1950, class M-1, 2-8-4..................215
#1959, class M-1, 2-8-4............211, 213
#1961, class M-1, 2-8-4..................214
#1967, class M-1, 2-8-4..................208
#1974, class M-1, 2-8-4..................212
#1978, class M-1, 2-8-4.......211, 213, 215
#1980, class M-1, 2-8-4..................215
#1991, class M-1, 2-8-4..................214

Louisville & Wadley Railroad................108

Missouri-Illinois Railroad..................113
Locomotives:
#1, 2-8-0...............................112
#7, 2-8-0...............................115
#24, 2-8-0..............................115
#154, 2-8-0, leased M.P.................114
#625, Gas-electric......................114

Page

Missouri-Kansas-Texas 9
Locomotives:
#396, 4-6-2............................. 41

Missouri Pacific Lines...................... 9
Locomotives:
#1121, class BK-63, 2-8-4...............257
#1449, class MK-63, 2-8-2............... 21
#1716, class SF-63, 2-10-2.............. 20
#2208, class N-73, 4-8-4...............254
#2210, class N-73, 4-8-4............... 18
#2213, class N-73, 4-8-4............... 10
#2348, class TN-61, 4-6-0.............. 22
#5326, class MT-75, 4-8-2.............. 19
#5344, class MT-73, 4-8-2.............. 20
#6618, class P-73, 4-6-2...............259

Montour Railroad
Locomotives:
#35, 2-8-2..............................111

New York Central System.................10, 93
Locomotives:
#2090, class H10b, 2-8-2............... 29
#2917, class L2d, 4-8-2................ 23
#2943, class L2d, 4-8-2................256
#3000, class L3, 4-8-2................. 24
#4909, class K5b, 4-6-2................ 29
#4915, class K5b, 4-6-2................ 26
#5378, class J1d, 4-6-4................ 27
#5387, class J1d, 4-6-4................252
#6000, class S-1, 4-8-4................ 92
#6009, class S-1a, 4-8-4............... 94
#6025, class S-1a, 4-8-4............... 95

Nickel Plate Road.........................131
Locomotives:
#706, class S-1, 2-8-4..................136
#713, class S-1, 2-8-4..................156
#722, class S-1, 2-8-4..................156
#730, class S-1, 2-8-4..................137
#747, class S-2, 2-8-4..................135
#768, class S-2, 2-8-4.............130, 134
#814, class S-4, 2-8-4..................139

Norfolk & Western Roanoke Coal Chute........157

Norfolk & Western Railway...................131
Locomotives:
#605, class J, 4-8-4....................143
#611, class J, 4-8-4....................145
#1207, class A, 2-6-6-4.................138
#1213, class A, 2-6-6-4.................140
#1225, class A, 2-6-6-4.................140

Norfolk & Western Railway (*Continued*)
  #2088, class Y-4, 2-8-8-2...................142
  #2153, class Y-6, 2-8-8-2...................141
  #2168, class Y-6a, 2-8-8-2.................135

Northern Alberta Railway
  Locomotives:
  #52, 2-10-0.....................................237
  #161, 4-6-2....................................236

Northern Pacific
  Locomotives:
  #1806, class W-3, 2-8-2............... 37
  #2677, class A-4, 4-8-4................... 38
  #2682, class A-5, 4-8-4................... 37
  #5005, class Z-5, 2-8-8-4................ 39
  #5120, class Z-6, 4-6-6-4............... 39

Ontario Northland Railway
  Locomotives:
  #1102, 4-8-4..................................238

Pennsylvania Railroad.....................10, 63
  Locomotives:
  #1753, class I-1s 2-10-0................ 62
  #4241, class I-1s, 2-10-0.............64, 65
  #4345, class I-1s, 2-10-0................ 62
  #4554, class I-1s, 2-10-0................ 64
  #5482, class K-4s, 4-6-2................ 49
  #5499, class K-4s, 4-6-2................ 49
  #5500, class T-1, 4-4-4-4................ 43
  #6171, class J-1a, 2-10-4................ 45
  #6469, class J-1a, 2-10-4..............219
  #6704, class M-1a, 4-8-2.............46, 47
  #6861, class M-1, 4-8-2................ 44
  #6907, class M-1a, 4-8-2.............46, 47

Pittsburgh & Lake Erie.......................117
  Locomotives:
  #9406, class A2a, 2-8-4................. 13
  #9507, class H9b, 2-8-2..................260

Prescott & Northwestern
  Locomotives:
  #17, 2-8-2.....................................104

Reading Railroad.............................220
  Locomotives:
  #1817, class N-1-d, 2-8-8-0.............. 16
  #2114, class T-1, 4-8-4..................220
  #2119, class T-1, 4-8-4..................221

Rutland Railroad
  Locomotives:
  #85, class K-2, 4-6-2..................... 12
  #92, class L-1, 4-8-2..................... 11

Smoky Mountain Railroad.....................97
  Locomotives:
  #110, 4-6-2....................................105

Soo Line
  Locomotives:
  #5003, class O-20, 4-8-4................. 54

Southern Pacific Lines.......................189
  Locomotives:
  #9, 4-6-0, 3-foot gauge...................197
  #18, 4-6-0, 3-foot gauge.............196, 197
  #3801, class AC-9, 2-8-8-4..............194
  #4159, class AC-7, 4-8-8-2..............194
  #4181, class AC-8, 4-8-8-2..............195
  #4257, class AC-11, 4-8-8-2..............190
  #4432, class GS-4, 4-8-4..............188
  #4455, class GS-4, 4-8-4..............192
  #4459, class GS-4, 4-8-4..............193
  #5012, class SP-1, 4-10-2..............191

Southern Railway............................. 9
  Locomotives:
  #1317, class Ps2, 4-6-2................... 31

St. Louis-San Francisco Railway.............. 67
  Locomotives:
  #1044, 4-6-2................................ 66
  #1309, 2-8-0................................ 69
  #1500, 4-8-2................................ 68

St. Louis-Southwestern
  Locomotives:
  #664, class G-O, 4-6-0.....................241
  #819, class L-1, 4-8-4................... 42

Sylvania Central............................. 97
  Locomotives:
  #103, 4-6-0..............................106, 107

Tuskegee Railroad
  Locomotives:
  #101, 2-6-2..................................103

Union Pacific.......................159, 177, 231
  Locomotives:
  #808, 4-8-4..................................165
  #822, 4-8-4..............................164, 169
  #825, 4-8-4..................................168
  #829, 4-8-4..................................199
  #830, 4-8-4.................................. 2
  #832, 4-8-4..................................160
  #833, 4-8-4..................230, 232, 233
  #835, 4-8-4.................................. 2
  #836, 4-8-4..................................163
  #837, 4-8-4..................230, 232, 233

Union Pacific *(Continued)*
  #844, 4-8-4..............................168
  #2223, 2-8-2.............................162
  #2888, 4-6-2.............................158
  #3709, 4-6-6-4...........................163
  #3713, 4-6-6-4...........................162
  #3803, 4-6-6-4...........................171
  #3805, 4-6-6-4...........................174
  #3823, 4-6-6-4...........................170
  #3941, 4-6-6-4.......................180, 182
  #3947, 4-6-6-4...........................161
  #3956, 4-6-6-4...........................183
  #3985, 4-6-6-4...........................158
  #3995, 4-6-6-4...........................161
  #4001, 4-8-4.............................180
  #4002, 4-8-8-4.......................158, 178
  #4003, 4-8-8-4...........................181
  #4005, 4-8-8-4...........................184
  #4007, 4-8-8-4...........................264
  #4013, 4-8-8-4...........................185
  #4014, 4-8-8-4...........................187
  #4015, 4-8-8-4...........................179
  #4016, 4-8-8-4...........................180
  #4017, 4-8-8-4.......................182, 186
  #4018, 4-8-8-4.......................180, 182
  #4019, 4-8-8-4.......................176, 183
  #4022, 4-8-8-4.......................158, 264
  #5093, 4-10-2............................199
  #7039, 4-8-2.............................160
  #9006, 4-12-2............................175

  #9019, 4-12-2............................167
  #9035, 4-12-2............................172
  #9052, 4-12-2............................166
  #9080, 4-12-2............................173

Virginian Railway
  Locomotives:
  #710, class US-A, 2-8-8-2................ 25
  #722, class US-B, 2-8-8-2................ 23
  #211, class PA, 4-6-2....................246

Wabash Railroad............................. 9
  Locomotives:
  #573, class F-4, 2-6-0................... 50
  #701, class P-1, 4-6-4...................250
  #705, class P-1, 4-6-4...................251
  #706, class P-1, 4-6-4................... 51
  #2823, class M-1, 4-8-2.................. 50
  #2916, class O-1, 4-8-4.................. 48

Waldey Southern
  Locomotives:
  #53, 4-6-0...............................108

Western Maryland
  Locomotives:
  #1111, class I-2, 2-10-0................. 15
  #1211, class M-2, 4-6-6-4................ 15

Wrightsville & Tennille
  Locomotives:
  #43, 4-6-0...............................108